D1157689

SPEND YOUR LIFE WISELY™
THE DEEPER MEANING OF MONEY

ROSS LEVIN
CERTIFIED FINANCIAL PLANNER™

SPEND YOUR LIFE WISELY™

THE DEEPER MEANING OF MONEY

ROSS LEVIN
CERTIFIED FINANCIAL PLANNER™

Surnia Publishing
Edina, Minnesota

Cataloging-in-Publication Information

Cover Photo: Bridget Levin
Book Design: Paul Christenson, Blue Mammoth Design

Certified Financial Planner Board of Standards Inc. owns the
certification marks CFP®, CERTIFIED FINANCIAL
PLANNER™ and federally registered CFP (with flame design)
in the U.S., which it awards to individuals who successfully complete
CFP Board's initial and ongoing certification requirements.

The materials and process for printing this book are in accordance
with the Forest Stewardship Council and the Sustainable Forestry
Initiative program. Bang Printing is part of the Green Press Initiative.

First published in the United States of America in 2010 by Surnia
Publishing, 5200 West 73rd Street, Edina, MN 55439

Library of Congress Cataloging-in-Publication Data
Library of Congress Control Number: 2010926102
ISBN-13: 978-1450707022

Printed in the United States of America

FSC
Mixed Sources
Product group from well-managed
forests, controlled sources and
recycled wood or fiber
Cert no. BV-COC-930557
www.fsc.org
© 1996 Forest Stewardship Council

This book is dedicated to my wife, Bridget, and my daughters, Mimi and Vera, for consistently reinforcing the value of spending my life wisely.

There are many people for whom I am grateful and wish to acknowledge. First, my wife Bridget has served as my first editor for my columns. Not only does she improve them, but she also can veto them (a rarely used, but significantly important power). I also want to thank my editor from the Star Tribune, John Oslund, for giving me the opportunity to express my unaltered views in a forum that reaches far more people than I would otherwise reach on my own.

Laura Purdie Salas, Suzy Ridenour, and Todd Gruenig previewed these columns to insure that their grammar and content were appropriate. Kathy Longo, a business partner for ten years, and Wil Heupel, my co-founder of Accredited Investors Inc., have supported my writings and encouraged me to continue doing so. And lastly, I am grateful to our clients, whose real life experiences continue to teach me lessons that I can share with all of you.

SPEND YOUR LIFE WISELY.™

My first monthly column appeared in the *Star Tribune* on February 8, 2004, and was based on Mahlon Hoagland's science book, *The Way Life Works*, to propose that:

"Life tends to optimize rather than maximize. To optimize means to achieve just the right amount—a value in the middle range between too much and too little."

I believe this is not only a fundamental concept of the natural world, but also of the financial planning world.

I had no idea when I wrote this first piece that I would be encouraged to become a monthly contributor to the newspaper. I did feel, though, that much of the existing writing about finance was about how to make more, have more, and do more; as if more was better. Twenty-five plus years in financial planning have taught me that more is simply more. The challenge for each of us is how we develop an approach to our money that is fully integrated with our lives. "More" can often get in the way of these efforts. My columns offer a perspective on how to make money play its proper role in our lives.

Over the years, I have received hundreds of notes from people who have read what I have written and have been touched in some way by the work. Some were going through painful life experiences such as the loss of a job or loved one, and this non-traditional financial column helped them see things in a different and more hopeful way. Others wrote at times when the markets were the most turbulent and expressed that my words gave them a sense of relief. Many simply said thank you for helping them remember to Spend Your Life Wisely.™

I hope that by creating a book of some of my columns that have generated the most feedback, it will enable more of you to thoughtfully look at your own financial situations. Are they consistent with the things that matter most to you?

SPEND YOUR LIFE WISELY.™
Ross Levin, CFP®
January, 2010

"In our day-to-day world we find ourselves both struggling to absorb the latest financial news, studying the business pages before heading off to work, and also trying to find peace through a connection with the very heart of reality, that presence whom most of us call "God." We stretch across considerable intellectual and spiritual distances seeking a fulfillment and security and trying to be good stewards of our lives, responsive to the needs of others. It is rare to find companions on this journey who ably bring all of this together with intelligence, good humor and competence. Ross Levin can be counted to do so and, through this collection of his articles, reminds us that he is one of life's wonderful, sage companions. His writings assure us that, with this kind of help, we can find better ways to make decisions and to understand why they are better."

Mary McNamara
President, United Theological Seminary of the
Twin Cities

"In his writing and his professional life, Ross Levin manages to be a savvy and intelligent financial advisor, a sensitive and insightful depth psychologist and a soulful and wise philosopher/poet, all at the same time—a truly rare and winning combination. Plus, he's very successful at what he does. Listen to what he says. I do."

Eric Utne
Founder, *Utne Reader*

"Now more than ever people are seeking competent, thoughtful and insightful financial advice. For years Ross Levin has been doing just that as he helps people sort through and plan for all the complexities of money and life. This collection of Ross' columns will help smooth your road to financial happiness and well-being."

Nathan Dungan
Author

TABLE
OF
CONTENTS

1. Discovering Life's Meaning **1**

Winning Life's Jackpot 3

Threads of Meaning 9

Stay True 15

Reflections on the Riches We Leave Behind 23

Six-Word Memoirs 29

2. Choosing Hope and Gratitude **35**

False Fears 37

The Price of Worry 43

Trade-Offs 49

Living with Grace 55

Connections 63

**3. Considering Family Matters
and Money** **71**

The Art of Perception 73

The Value of Struggle 79

3. Considering Family Matters and Money (continued)

Gains and Losses   85

Real Retirement   91

What's Your Legacy?   97

4. Exploring Business and Financial Styles 103

Money Style   105

Delusions   109

True Self   115

5. Making Sound Financial Decisions 121

Too Bad to Be True   123

Choices   129

In the Moment   135

Perfect Segue   141

Spring for a Guide   147

Unpredictability   153

Timing the Market   157

Biography   163

General Reading List   165

Books Mentioned List   169

Discovering Life's Meaning

There are really only two purposes for your money—to spend it or to give it away. We continue to trade our days for dollars. While we may work for fulfillment, many of us are also working so that we can buy things that we think we want. We buy these things because we hope that they make us feel happier.

In working with hundreds of people over the years, there has been very little relationship between owning stuff and happiness. What has been consistent, though, is that those who invested in a much bigger life through relationships, philanthropy, honest self-assessment, and family seemed to be the most resilient and, ultimately, the most satisfied.

There is a poem by Jelaluddin Rumi, a 13th-century Sufi mystic:

I have lived on the lip
of insanity, wanting to know reasons,
knocking on a door. It opens.
I've been knocking from the inside.

Hopefully some of the columns in this section will help you also to see inside.

Winning Life's Jackpot

I occasionally do something that no rational financial planner would ever do. When the Powerball gets above a certain amount, I buy a ticket. This is ridiculous on so many levels I hardly know where to start.

What is most nuts is that when I buy the ticket, I begin to negotiate with God. I don't pray to win the lottery—I sort of feel like that would be a spiritual infraction. Instead I make deals with regard to how much of my winnings will be used to establish a charitable foundation instead of being spent on my family's prosperity.

The chances of my winning the lottery are less than Miley Cyrus' chances of winning an Oscar. Yet I find myself constantly changing the deal that I make with God regarding what we keep versus what we donate to society.

I write this because I am realizing that we are entering a cycle of fear and greed that is similar to what many people experienced in the late 1990s. When it comes to money, fear and greed are really the same thing. When stock markets are going up (as they have pretty consistently done since the fourth quarter of 2002), investors are mostly concerned with grabbing the biggest return they can, regardless of what they ultimately plan to do with their money. When markets are going down, investors tend to worry that they'll end up with nothing, changing their whole picture of the future.

Yet the simple truth is that you can't have it both ways. Strong stock gains looked like loaves of bread to the starving investors of 2003. Now these same investors not only take them for granted but want more and more.

Fear and greed both represent emotional responses to an imagined future. And they both represent scarcity. When I am mentally scaling back on my lottery generosity it is because I am feeling scared that I won't have enough—even though what I would be keeping (assuming I won) is way more than I am likely ever to have. Most shockingly, when I really stop to think about what I already have without winning the lottery, it is enough.

Rather than talk with you about the virtues of asset allocation and diversification, I want to instead focus on perspective. In his book *The Heart Aroused—Poetry and the Preservation of the Soul in Corporate America*, David Whyte wrote:

> "When all the things we want beyond our reach move slowly within our reach, it is easy to feel good about life. But if our sense of well-being becomes dependent on the constant delivery of goods to our door, we experience a sense of loss when the supply suddenly dries up, or we no longer perceive it has the same value."

Our well-being does not depend on one year's investment returns. It depends on how we wish to spend and value our resources. Well-being is not about portfolio values, it is about personal values.

Try this exercise:

Must have. Create a list of those things that you feel that you must have. These are not wants; these are the things that are necessary for you to live your life. This list may include things like your home, education for your children, your pets, service to the community, your free time. Beside each of these "must haves," write a brief description of why it is important to you.

Don't need or want. Next, write a list of things in your life that you have but don't really need or want. This could be old clothing or other unused items, organizations for which you volunteer, maybe even your job. Beside each of these, write a brief description of what you will gain by giving it up.

Rarely think about. Last, create a list of things that consume your resources but that you hardly ever think about. Maybe it's eating out, or constantly checking e-mails, or incessantly and needlessly checking your portfolio online. Write next to these why you value them. If you can't come up with a legitimate reason, move it to the "don't-need-or-want" grouping.

When you are done, you'll be able to see those conscious choices that help you and those that have been ineffective for you. You will also see the unconscious choices that add little value to your life. My suspicion is that you will find many of your former wants in both the "don't-need-or-want" and the "rarely-think-about" lists.

What would be different if you had not used your resources on those things, but on your "must-have" list instead? You most likely would experience less fear because you would have more of the things in your life that matter. And you would want less because you will see how fleeting those wants are.

When I remember to do this exercise, I realize that I already have won the lottery.

SPEND YOUR LIFE WISELY.™
THIS COLUMN ORIGINALLY APPEARED IN THE MINNEAPOLIS *Star Tribune* ON FEBRUARY 18, 2007.

Threads of Meaning

On a recent family trip, we were offered 40 camels and a pottery business for the hand in marriage of one of our twin teenage daughters. While there have been one or two days in her life when we may have considered a dowry of far less—say, a one-eyed cat and a cold slushy, we rejected the proposal immediately.

After the last 12 months, I am more aware than ever that things cannot replace what truly matters in life.

Due to the erratic year in the markets, I had basically put much of my life on hold. I felt that I couldn't be out of the office for five minutes given all the turbulence in the economy and my perceived need of constant client contact and hand-holding.

In retrospect, this decision was not one of the better ones I have made. The overdue family vacation, from which we just returned, has not only refreshed me, it has helped to refocus me—which will help me better serve our clients.

William Stafford, in his poem "The Way It Is," wrote:

> There's a thread that you follow. It goes among
> things that change. But it doesn't change.
> People wonder about what you are pursuing.
> You have to explain about the thread.
> But it is hard for others to see.
> While you hold it you can't get lost.
> Tragedies happen; people get hurt
> or die: and you suffer and get old.
> Nothing you do can stop time's unfolding.
> You don't ever let go of the thread.

Stafford's words hit home for me and they pose a fundamental question upon which all of your financial planning should be based: What is the thread of your life?

It may be many things, but it certainly is not money. Money can only be a byproduct. If you are a successful surgeon, your thread may be saving the lives of others. You may be paid well for it. But if you are a social worker, your thread may also be saving the lives of others.

Maybe you don't get paid quite so well. Does that make the meaning of your work any less important?

For many of us, our financial worlds have changed. We simply don't have as much money as we had a year ago. We are more aware of how tenuous certain aspects of our lives are. If we pay attention, not only do our balance sheets look different, but our work does as well. But this does not mean that times are worse, it only means that they are different.

Some of the suffering that we are experiencing can bring us closer to our thread. It is easy to get swept along when things are going well. We build grand plans with great visions. We put aside family in the name of earning more to provide for the family. We place enormous pressures on our portfolios to grow so that we can buy a better or a bigger or a different life.

One of my good friends was diagnosed and treated for cancer during the short time we were gone on vacation. This was someone whose thread has always been about connecting people with the resources that would help them enrich their lives. So it was no surprise that because his thread has been about service, the many people whose lives he touched rallied around him to help him get incredible medical care and treatment, and they will provide him and his family with ongoing encouragement and support. Time unfolds, tragedies happen, people get hurt. Our thread endures.

If you are rapidly racing to recapture what you have lost, now is a good time to rediscover what you already have. The market is going to come back to previous levels, probably more slowly than we hope. The economic climate is going to improve, but not without its stumbles. It will be very tempting to anticipate the next correction and its ensuing rebound. But the strength of this current rebound should have taught you that predicting short-term market movements is nearly impossible.

Rather than attempting this, if you need some money in the short term, sell some of your stocks. If you don't need money, then rebalance. But far more important than getting this timing just right is rekindling the fire of what you want to do with this stage of your life. If you were to strip away all the accoutrements of the life that you have created, what is essential to you right in this moment? If you have found yourself in a holding pattern, prepare to launch.

SPEND YOUR LIFE WISELY.™

THIS COLUMN ORIGINALLY APPEARED IN THE
MINNEAPOLIS *Star Tribune* ON JUNE 28, 2009.

Stay True

In his poem, "The Contract," William Ayot wrote:

A word from the led
And in the end we follow them—
Not because we are paid,
Not because we might see some advantage,
Not because of the things they have
    accomplished,
Not even because of the dreams they dream
But simply because of who they are:
The man, the woman, the leader, the boss
Standing up there when the wave hits the rock,
Passing out faith and confidence like life
    jackets,
Knowing the currents, holding the doubts,
Imagining the delights and terrors of every
    landfall:
Captain, pirate, and parent by turns,
The bearer of our countless hopes and
    expectations.

We give them our trust. We give them our
    effort.
What we ask in return is that they stay true.

I read this as I was going through the book, *Leading
from Within—Poetry That Sustains the Courage to
Lead,* by Sam Intrator and Megan Scribner. The amount
of responsibility that rests on our shoulders is stagger-
ing. Clients and staff give us their trust and their effort.
And what they ask in return is that we stay true.

Here is your chance to escape. If you don't wish to
explore who you are and whether you should be doing
what you are doing, then stop reading this. Once you get
past this paragraph, there is no turning back.

I have one simple question for you—can you stay true?

One of our staff members said to me over lunch, "You
always talk about loyalty. It was easy to say that when
the markets were going up and the money was coming in. But all of your actions over the last year have
shown that you really mean it." He may have been
referring to the letter that we sent to each of our clients that discussed how even though our fee income

has dropped as significantly as their portfolios, we were going to hold staffing steady. He could have been thinking about how, during the October 2008 trading crunch, which resulted in numerous trade errors, we unquestioningly covered the losses associated with them for our clients. Or maybe he was talking about how we continued our policy of five volunteer days a year that each employee can use for a charity of his or her choice. Could he have been commenting on the weekly e-mail updates to clients, the expert webinars, or the emphasis on planning that we were providing?

What Being True Isn't

I struggle with staying true every day. Sometimes I feel like my existence depends on trying to have my words and my deeds align. When I get angry with my teenage daughters or take a client's fear as an indictment of me, I know that I am not being true. When I kick out a sarcastic e-mail or don't speak up with a staff member who has frustrated me, I see how I am not being authentic.

In many ways, though, everything depends on being true. The false gods of modern portfolio theory or absolute return strategies have been replaced by the new deities of fixed annuities or bonds. Research on sustainable withdrawal rates may be quantitatively correct and qualitatively useless.

Clients are sitting across from us and asking the only question that ever needs to be answered: "Is my family going to be okay?"

If your immediate response is, "Of course," you are not being true. If you tell the clients that they need to make dramatic changes, you are not being true. Being true is helping clients understand that these are very difficult times and that you are going to be there with them, sharing in the difficulty and trying to figure out solutions that are more good than bad. Being true is helping clients to understand that some things are going to work out well, and others not so well. We are the bearers of our clients' countless hopes and expectations. It is tempting to assure them by quoting historic returns or giving in to their fears (and your own) by selling out of everything.

Every time you speak with certainty, you are no longer being true.

There are people out there who will emphatically say that things are this way or that way. And they are always right until they are wrong. They are not being true.

My Process for Staying True

I want to share with you my personal process for trying to stay true.

Every morning I wake up early, start a pot of coffee, and walk our two dogs, who are always excited to see me. Having twin 16-year-old daughters and a wife of 25 years, sometimes the dogs are the only beings in the house excited to see me. I try to think through things for this 20 minutes. Sometimes I find myself getting irritated at something I am thinking about and I note it.

When I get back, I pour myself a cup of coffee, sit down at my desk, and begin to read. I read three types of things: a daily affirmation, a spiritual book, and a book of meaning (currently, for example, the poems of Rilke). I then open my journal and I begin to write. I write about anything I thought about on my walk. I write about things that I am trying to sort out personally or with work. I write about what my role has been in anything that is not going particularly well and what I need to do to make amends. I try to think about ways in which my ego is getting in the way of work or relationships.

I can't tell you the number of times that this ritual has helped me realize that I have responsibility for some of the things about which I was blaming others. I also can tell you that I begin my day with a clear head, no lingering resentments, and an action plan for what I need to do to be true. There are many days where I don't follow through with everything that I thought I needed to do, but my daily writing means that I can't escape things for long.

Transparency, Discernment, and Presence
At work, I try to stay true through transparency. Our quarterly all-staff retreats help open up issues that may be unresolved. Our monthly calls help the principals work through things. We are trying to emphasize feedback with everyone closer to an event's occurrence rather than letting issues linger. I regularly acknowledge how fallible I am.

I am more committed than ever to the business because in my heart I believe that we can make a big difference in the lives of our clients and our staff.

With prospective clients, I try to distinguish those who are leaving their advisors because of things that would have happened had they been with us—like not predicting this market—from those who want to leave because they were not handled the way we would handle them. Even though we could use the new business, I don't want to take on the first type of client. I wish to fill my firm with the latter.

With existing clients, I am trying to listen to their fear and their hurt and their frustration. I am trying to keep the focus on their needs and not to get defensive. It can be very challenging. Some days I am better at this than others.

At home, I am trying to be present. I am not frequently checking e-mails or going to the computer. I am trying to stay off the computer completely on weekends. I am getting regular exercise. I am reading good books. I am writing appreciation notes to those who have done something special for me and condolence notes to those who are going through difficult times.

I don't know what is going to happen. I only know that I can handle what comes my way. And I can only do that if I am true.

SPEND YOUR LIFE WISELY.™

REPRINTED WITH PERMISSION BY THE FINANCIAL PLANNING ASSOCIATION, *Journal of Financial Planning*, APRIL 2009, ROSS LEVIN, "STAYING TRUE."

For more information on the Financial Planning Association, please visit www.fpanet.org or call 1-800-322-4237.

Reflections on the Riches We Leave Behind

I was about to give a speech and, while listening to my host's introduction, I realized that it sounded like my obituary. He talked about what I had accomplished, but he made no mention of who I really was.

The words used to describe me were ones that I had hoped would give me credibility with my audience. Then I got to thinking that some of our problems with money are also because we allow it to define us. We become our possessions or our balance sheets.

As we are "dying" from what the markets have done to our hard-earned savings, maybe we need to take a moment and a deep breath to think about how good we really have it. I thought I would share some lessons that I have learned from friends and acquaintances who have passed away. From these lessons, I hope that I can live my real obituary—especially the typical husband and father part.

He had a sense of gratitude. One of our seemingly healthiest clients died relatively unexpectedly of a very fast-growing cancer. I do not recall a meeting that I ever had with this person when he and his wife did not in some way express gratitude for the life that they had. Even as the cancer claimed his body, he continued to appreciate all that he had in his life. As sad as it was for his wife to lose him, she would continue to comment on the many great years that they had had together.

In his book *Thanks! How Practicing Gratitude Can Make You Happier,* Robert Emmons described the long-lasting effects of gratitude:

> "[G]rateful thinking fosters the savoring of positive life experiences . . . may directly counteract the process by which our happiness level returns to its set-point, and makes it harder to take for granted and adapt to our blessings."

While many of us have been dealt difficult hands, some almost impossibly difficult, a sense of gratitude for what is going right can counterbalance those things that are not working out as planned.

He gave to those from whom he expected nothing in return. One of my friends was telling me about his father's obituary guest book. While he was alive, his father had left his wallet in a gas station in a small town in central Minnesota. When the attendant mailed the wallet back with a note, the father sent a thank-you note and a gift basket. While this incident happened several years ago, the attendant noticed the obituary and described the story in the guest book. The reciprocal goodness from these actions left life-long impressions with both people.

Emmons said that "life is about giving, receiving and repaying." While we spend so much time focusing on the big things, it is often the little things that create life's richness.

He was interested in much and many. I recently went to a funeral that was filled to the rafters with people who came to pay their last respects to their coach and teacher who had passed away. Most significant to me were the varied walks of life represented by the people who packed the church. In addition to his family, attendees included kids he taught and coached, friends with whom he hunted and fished, fellow parishioners, and dozens of others in whose life he took an interest. This was a person who had many passions and was also passionate about others. The crowded worship hall was a testament to how much impact we can have in our daily interactions.

He lightened others' loads. One of our clients who passed away from ALS kept us laughing from beginning to end of each meeting. Even when the illness prevented him from communicating, he never lost the twinkle in his eye. While he was a very successful and even intense business owner, he saw the humor and lightness in much of life. The laughter with which he surrounded himself helped everyone through the trauma of his terrible disease.

She recognized how connected we all are. One of our clients was a woman who died of cancer. She had spent her life volunteering for a number of causes. She viewed her time of service as an acknowledgment of all that she had been given in her lifetime and as a way to support those who had less. Emmons wrote:

> "We all begin life dependent on others, and most of us end life dependent on others. In between,

we have roughly sixty years or so of unacknowl-
edged dependency. The human condition is such
that throughout life, not just at the beginning
and end, we are profoundly dependent on other
people."

This has been a difficult year financially for many of us.
But the riches that we leave behind often have nothing
to do with money.

SPEND YOUR LIFE WISELY.™
THIS COLUMN ORIGINALLY APPEARED IN THE
MINNEAPOLIS *Star Tribune* ON NOVEMBER 22, 2008.

Six-Word Memoirs

Ernest Hemingway once was asked to write a book in six words. To some, it may be his best work: "For sale: baby shoes, never worn."

I have imagined many stories about these six words. Is this about a failed pregnancy? Is it about people who wanted to conceive yet were unable to do so? Is it about grandparents being kept away from their grandchild?

This got me thinking. People are always asking me what financial planning books I would recommend. Now, since times are a little tight, rather than have you go out and buy a book, I have written a few six-word soliloquies based on lessons learned from clients.

Owned a ton. Crushed by it. Of course, the central tenet of financial planning is to pay yourself first by spending less than you make and saving a portion of all that you earn. While this is sound advice, it really is not complete.

We have had clients come into our offices who have saved over their lives, built up nice nest eggs, and also have spent money on many things that they thought mattered. Over time, those things mattered less, yet they were reluctant to give up something that they already had.

How many possessions do you have because you think that you will use them someday? Little things like the never-used cross-country skis or big things like the cabin for which you no longer make time may be better used by someone else and relieve you of the guilt that can come from overabundance.

A friend of mine sold her car several years ago and now walks or takes public transportation almost everywhere she goes. Once or twice a month she rents a car for the weekend to do some chores for which she would rather drive herself. Not only does this strategy save her money on buying a car, gas, insurance and upkeep, but I guarantee that she gets more exercise than I do.

Write down your expenses. Include items bought that you are not using and what this ownership costs you. If you sell these, you may be shocked at how little the sacrifice is for the gains ahead of you.

Risked much. Lost much. Gained more. Whether it is the stock market, choosing a spouse, moving to a new home—or almost any major decision we make—we must accept the risk of things not going exactly as we had planned in order to reap the rewards of a richer existence.

I know a developer who recently filed personal bankruptcy on a business that had been tremendously successful. He said that there are people he runs into who still thank him for the homes he built them. While he certainly did not want things to end this way, he loves the positive impact that he had on his customers.

Don't try to avoid risk; manage it. Niebuhr's Serenity Prayer encourages us to "accept the things [we] cannot change and the courage to change the things [we] can." The things that go wrong help us appreciate those that are going right.

Kept looking back. Couldn't move forward. While Santayana taught us that "Those who cannot remember the past are condemned to repeat it," he should have created the corollary: "Those who live in the past have no future."

It is important to distinguish how the past can guide you from how it can control you. If you lost money in the stock market and vow to never invest in stocks again, you are being controlled. If you decide that you want to better understand your risk tolerance or your asset allocation, you are being guided. Our most successful clients are those who have learned from their mistakes, not those who wallow in them.

She had little; more than imaginable. If you do nothing else before the start of this year, I suggest you sit down for at least 15 minutes (yes, set a timer), and write down those things for which you are grateful. We get so caught up in life's volatility that we don't focus on those little things that have an impact on us. As you do this, think about what you can do for others.

I get so moved by handwritten notes I receive, that I try to write them as well. One of my clients drives around town with sandwiches and socks to give to those people at the stoplights who appear homeless. Our family gives 10 percent of our earnings to causes that we care deeply about. Maybe it's unlikely that we can change the world, but we can each certainly improve upon someone's world.

SPEND YOUR LIFE WISELY.™

THIS COLUMN ORIGINALLY APPEARED IN THE MINNEAPOLIS *Star Tribune* ON DECEMBER 27, 2009.

2

Choosing Hope and Gratitude

"If the only prayer you ever say in your entire life is thank you, it will be enough."

—*Friar Meister Eckhart*

We live in a world where abundance is all around us. We may complain about the car we drive without recognizing that not only do we live in a place where getting around is so easy, but we own the mode of transportation to do so. We are constantly thinking about what we have lost, but paying little attention to all that we have gained.

There is a story of two young twin girls – one a pessimist, the other an optimist. On their eighth birthday, their parents opened the door to their rooms. The pessimist's room was filled to the top with wrapped presents. With a dour look she turned around and said, "There must be a catch." The optimist's room was filled to the top with horse manure. When they opened the door, their daughter squealed and jumped to the top of the pile, digging furiously. When asked what she was doing, she said, "With all this horse manure, there must be a pony in here somewhere."

One of the things that we tell our clients is that the only thing that we can promise is uncertainty and our ability to help them through it. And the best antidote for uncertainty is a real appreciation for what is and a belief in what may be.

False Fears

I will tell you the most scared I've ever been.

Several years ago, when I was walking back with my popcorn during intermission at the drive-in movie double feature of the original *The Hills Have Eyes* and *The Texas Chainsaw Massacre*, my wife jumped out at me from behind our car. I threw the popcorn in the air, jumped in the vehicle, and started to drive away, almost leaving my wife and taking the speaker with me.

Yet there is a difference between being *scared* and being *afraid*. Scared seems to be a reaction to an immediate event. Afraid seems to be a more all-encompassing, even suffocating, feeling. During these difficult times, I think that it is normal to feel scared; I caution you against being afraid.

Each of us reacts in our own way to the events around us. These days you can respond to bank failures, a housing collapse, unemployment, the stock market, or the tone of the current political campaigns. But when we move from the immediacy of our scared reaction toward a general state of being, we are now afraid.

In his book *The Science of Fear*, Daniel Gardner wrote:

> "[N]ews stories routinely say there is a possibility of something bad happening without providing a meaningful sense of how likely that bad thing is."

We are not about to enter another Great Depression. In fact, Federal Reserve Chairman Ben Bernanke's playbook for handling this current crisis is a result of his extensive study of that terrible time. While we are in a global recession, it is not a global meltdown. If we aren't overleveraged with our investments, we are suffering from a Three-Mile-Island-like leak, not a Chernobyl event. This distinction is important—one was a scare, the other a disaster.

Governments around the world have stepped in to unlock credit. Our bank deposits are insured up to $250,000. While some of us have lost jobs, the unemployment rate is significantly lower than it was through much of the 1980s, a time of tremendous stock market growth. Times are tough right now, but times have been tough before. We are going to see some fundamental changes because of this economic cycle, but neither this cycle nor the changes will be permanent. Things will keep changing. The thing to think about is what you can do until things get better. We don't know when the markets will improve, although they certainly will. But there are several steps you can take right now.

Review your cash flow. This is the time when you can perform your own line-item veto of extraneous things that are simply not making a big difference in your life. Little things like changing your cable television package, bringing your lunch to work, eating at home more often, or reviewing your insurance deductibles don't seem like much, but many of them add up to some pretty significant savings. This also is a great time to strongly negotiate on larger purchases that you don't wish to put off.

Rebalance your portfolios. You should now be adding to your stock position in your retirement plans. Your bonds have most likely fallen less than your stocks, so you want to calibrate back to your original ratio. Also, this is a great time to do tax swaps of mutual funds in your nonretirement accounts. If you are holding a mutual fund with a loss, you can sell it and buy a similar but not identical fund. This will keep you invested but give you a tax write-off.

Talk to people. Many of us are experiencing similar feelings. Don't go it alone. Your spiritual home may be offering support groups. Encourage leaders at your work environment to create a place to talk. This is an important time not to isolate yourself. If you are spending your days surfing the Net or glued to CNN, you are filling your head with information way scarier than *Texas Chainsaw Massacre*'s Leatherface.

Remember that fear is false evidence appearing real. Time spent in the land of "what-could-happen" deprives you of your life today. While you need to create plans for different scenarios, it won't help to wait for them to come.

I was talking with a friend about his daughter who had returned to an active life after surgery. She went through extensive rehab and is now fully ready to participate in sports again. She will either get injured or she won't. If she gets injured again, they will deal with it. If she doesn't, then they can enjoy her athleticism with her. But they can't stop living because of what might happen. None of us really knows what the future holds. Uncertainty is our only certainty.

Reach out to others in need. Give a little something to charity. You would be surprised at how this will loosen some of the money grip that has its hold on you.

It isn't a question of if things will get better, it is merely a question of when. Stick around for the second movie. It probably won't be nearly as scary.

SPEND YOUR LIFE WISELY.™
THIS COLUMN ORIGINALLY APPEARED IN THE MINNEAPOLIS *Star Tribune* ON OCTOBER 25, 2008.

SPEND YOUR LIFE WISELY

The Price of Worry

One of our two cats is quite hefty. Not so big as to cause concern, but certainly of a size that we often confuse her for one of our dogs when we hear her traipsing around the house. While it may seem obvious, we discovered that she achieved this state by eating her own helping of cat food as well as much of our other cat's portion. This proves the adage, "What you feed grows."

The news is filled with economic horror stories. Unemployment in Minnesota is nearly 7 percent, and our state deficit is more than $5 billion. Companies are not only downsizing, but some are disappearing.

Are you paralyzed in front of your television, radiated to a sickly pallor, numbly watching stock quotes cascade along the bottom of the screen as pundits above describe the impending apocalypse? Are you grabbing a paper bag into which you take deep breaths when you open your monthly brokerage statements?

Let me ask you two simple questions: What are you feeding and why are you feeding it? Many of you are gorging on fear and disappointment, feasting on the unknown as if it were haute cuisine. There is not a soul on earth who knows how TARP, TALF, or any other governmental acronym is going to turn out.

Commentator of the day Peter Schiff may have predicted much of the current economic malaise, but his investment accounts in 2008 were still rumored to lose around 40 percent. That's like Wile E. Coyote breathing a sigh of relief as he avoids being hit by a truck, only to be run over by a train.

The point is not to pick on Schiff, but to illustrate that no one will consistently have all the answers, and frankly, that is not what's really important, anyway.

It's time to stop dining on disaster and to figure a way to make the most of what's on your plate.

Dale Carnegie wrote his classic book, *How to Stop Worrying and Start Living*, in 1944—the year after the worst 15-year period for returns in stock market history. His advice is as timely today as it was then:

"The best possible way to prepare for tomorrow is to concentrate with all your intelligence, all your enthusiasm, on doing today's work superbly today."

Figure out what you can do and do it well. Focus on your own piece to create your own peace. Working hard at what you do best will feed your sense of fulfillment. Rather than worrying about losing your job, make yourself invaluable by demonstrating a tremendous effort. If you have lost your job, use this time to determine what a new career could look like or network like mad to land something else. Look for emerging sectors that may be more viable now. Things could certainly get worse for you, but tough times do not last. Most importantly, if you are not feeding worries about what could go wrong, you are instead creating a new game plan that gets you ready for the inevitable upturn.

A person I knew in high school recently wrote me to say that she had just lost her condo to foreclosure. The stress of trying to make payments while weaving a negative story about what losing her home would be like made things emotionally unbearable. After she lost the condominium, she was shocked at how she actually was able to adjust to her new life. Of course, it was not ideal, but she discovered that she could adapt. Her imagined doomsday scenario never matched the tenable reality of it.

For most of us, the worst is never going to happen. Carnegie quoted the 16th-century French philosopher Montaigne: "My life has been full of terrible misfortunes, most of which never happened." If things bounce back in a couple of years, ask yourself: Did you improve your life by obsessing over what could have gone wrong? In the meantime, think of concrete, creative ways to prepare yourself in case things don't improve before you need your money. Evaluate your spending, review your investments, enjoy your work in case you need to work longer, and focus on helping others less fortunate.

No matter what, we will work our way out of this economic predicament. I say this not because of a belief in governmental steps being taken, but in an abiding belief in equilibrium. Things stay good for a while and then go bad for a while. Rather than continuing to think about how awful things could get, pay attention to what is going right. The best thing that you can do today is to enjoy your own heaping plate of "now." It frankly is the only thing over which you truly have control.

SPEND YOUR LIFE WISELY.™
THIS COLUMN ORIGINALLY APPEARED IN THE MINNEAPOLIS *Star Tribune* ON FEBRUARY 21, 2009.

Trade-Offs

If a tree fell on our cabin and nobody heard it, would it make a noise?

Rather than ponder this deep philosophical question, I called our insurance guy. He was more interested in damage than in philosophy. After the 100-foot white pine, perched majestically between our dining room and our waterfront, took out part of our roof and porch, we were lamenting our loss. Overhearing this, one of our daughters piped up with, "Well, at least we can see the lake now."

She was right. Rather than focus on what we are losing, it is time to think about what we are gaining. Now that we can see the lake, our choices become easier.

Every prudent financial planning decision involves letting go of something good in order to get something better. The act of saving means that you give up some lifestyle today to live more comfortably tomorrow. More schooling means you give up time and income today to hopefully create more opportunity later.

These are obvious choices. But the more subtle choices are the ones from which a meaningful life is derived.

We can see the lake when we teach our children about money rather than either capriciously denying things that they request or impulsively buying them.

When our daughters turned 13 we put them on a monthly allowance from which they paid for their monthly entertainment, clothing, and all the other nonessential (to us, not necessarily to them) teen items.

Soon after this program began, they were going to summer camp. When they asked that we deposit enough money in the canteen for them to get sweatshirts, we suggested that this was an item that came out of their clothing budget. They returned from camp with great experiences and no new sweatshirts.

Trying to raise responsible teenagers means that we have to control our own impulses and treat the kids only on rare occasions.

We can see the lake when we are intentional with our gifting. There is a never-ending list of wants in life.

And every want that is satisfied often creates multiple new ones. After 25 years of financial planning, I can attest that the most satisfying way to curb these wants is through giving to others.

It is incredible to be in client meetings and watch moods change when we move the conversation from personal spending to charitable giving. While personal spending is always about wondering "will we have enough," philanthropy always involves recognizing what we already have. When they consciously increase their charitable giving, clients are in effect acknowledging that they have enough.

We can see the lake when we share with our family our life experiences. We have a client who has created his vision for the future on the Internet for friends and family to watch. Developing this vision forced him to focus on the things that he wanted to do with his life over the next several years; sharing it allows those closest to him to participate in these dreams. We never know how much time we have.

Seeing the lake doesn't come from thinking about your legacy, it comes from memorializing it. Think about having someone videotape you discussing what you have learned over the years and what you still hope to do and to learn. Don't worry about how it turns out. The simple act of recording it will mean more to your family than you could possibly imagine.

We can see the lake when we think about what our impact is on those around us. One of our clients died this year of complications involving ALS (also called Lou Gehrig's disease). Over the 19 months that he had the illness, we watched him come into our offices beginning with a slight limp, then with a cane, then pushing a walker, and eventually, being pushed in a wheelchair.

As his body continued to break down, his spirit never did. I am sure there were times when he was angry with his plight. I would think that he may have at times felt betrayed. But I can tell you that I never saw the twinkle leave his eye. He made everyone around him feel better for knowing him. And as I write this, with his memory permanently etched in my mind, I am not picturing our last meeting—when he could no longer move. I am vividly seeing his grace with all whom he encountered. He had that impact before the ALS, and he never lost it after he contracted the disease.

That white pine was beautiful, and I really appreciate its place in our life. But now we get to see the lake. Can you?

SPEND YOUR LIFE WISELY.™
THIS COLUMN ORIGINALLY APPEARED IN THE MINNEAPOLIS *Star Tribune* ON OCTOBER 21, 2007.

Living with Grace

This has been an unbelievably difficult year. I have lost more money through my investments than I made (according to my Social Security statement) during my first ten years *combined* of working! We are fielding phone calls from clients who are wondering whether they will have enough to (fill in the blank) (a) retire, (b) pay for their kids' schooling, (c) leave unfulfilling but lucrative work for a job with meaning, (d) all of the above, and more. My mother passed away in August at age 83 from a brain tumor diagnosed in January.

This is not a column about what is wrong with my world. I don't dismiss the daily professional and personal challenges that each of us confronts. It would be a terrible denial to act like everything is fine when it isn't. But it would be equally disingenuous to act like everything is falling apart when it isn't. This is a column about grace.

Messages in Life and Death

The week my mother's brain cancer was diagnosed, the 39-year-old daughter of one of our clients committed suicide. This gifted woman had struggled for years with bipolar disorder. Her parents, now in their seventies, had recoiled from late-night phone calls. In their minds, it was not if—but when—their daughter would decide she could not go on. Through the years, we laughed together, cried together, and came to grips with what we could and could not control. The church was packed for their daughter's funeral. Her brothers shared stories of how caring she was and how rich she made their lives. While the profound sadness of the moment filled the sanctuary, so did the wonder of her life spent on earth.

Shortly after my mother died, a 55-year-old doctor and his wife came to our office. I had known him through shared community involvement. He was here for professional reasons—he had been diagnosed with brain cancer and he wanted to be sure his financial house was in order. Sarah, from my firm, joined us for the meeting, and the four of us talked. We talked about family and love and loss and faith and fear. We talked about what things would look like if he was one of the few survivors from this type of cancer and what would happen if he wasn't. We shared big things and little things. He wanted the name of the person who cuts my hair.

He was just in again this week for our first meeting after hiring us. He and his wife had bought a tandem bike so they could ride the 14 miles together to and from his radiation treatments. The scar from the removed tumor was visible because of his hair loss. His wife blamed my haircutter. He was trying to arrange a flight to Duke University to begin his chemo treatment. We talked about them going to India next June with their teen-age daughters. But there is a chance he won't be alive in June.

Gratitude

Three things sit on my desk in my office. One is a rock with the Serenity Prayer inscribed on it: "God grant me the serenity to accept the things I cannot change; Courage to change the things I can; And the wisdom to know the difference." I have a small magnet that my daughters gave me for Father's Day a couple of years ago with Mahatma Gandhi's words: "We must be the change we wish to see in the world." And I have a card from the ancient mystic Rumi that says, "If it is love you are look-ing for, take a knife and cut off the head of fear."

There is so much going on and I have so much for which I am grateful. Here are a few things.

I am grateful for impermanence. The good times don't last but neither do the bad. What seems so important one moment is lost like the name of an acquaintance at a conference.

I am grateful for the things that last. While the world is constantly changing, some things seem to stick with us forever. I have had seemingly insignificant interactions that are indelibly carved into my brain. There are faces of certain people who showed me kindness that I can conjure up much more easily than those who have hurt me. Of course, I also have regret for things that I never said or things that I said out of emotion, but I have had far more good moments than bad ones.

I am grateful for a job where I can make a difference in peoples' lives. At times we make money for clients and other times we lose money for clients. But we are always trying to figure out how we can improve their lives. We don't always succeed, but any success we have had has led to those clients feeling good enough about their situation that they can go out and make a difference in the lives of others. We don't need to touch thousands of people to make a difference; we need only touch a few who in turn can go out and help others.

I am grateful for my mistakes. Unexamined, mistakes are not very useful. But almost tortuously turning them over in my brain and my journal has helped me discover meaning and context and a connection with others.

I am grateful for risk. Getting married, having children, starting a business, becoming involved in activities; these were all things whose results have been unpredictable. Some of the things I have done turned out terribly—for example, I failed as president of a brokerage firm in my late twenties. But accepting risk is rejecting fear. I have no idea what the future will bring, but I know I can handle its uncertainty.

I am grateful for optimization rather than maximization. In spite of what we heard during this political season, there are very few situations where there is only one correct answer. Multiple truths are the natural consequence of a complex world. I have spent a lifetime trying to figure out not how to get it right, but simply how to get it.

I am grateful for giving. The most enduring things are those that come back the more you give them away.

Love, hope, and charity disappear as you cling to them. As I stare age 50 in its unblinking face, the regenerative virtues are not all that matter, but they are certainly the things that matter when things seem to be falling apart.

I am grateful for choice. I get to decide how I am going to trade my days for dollars or experiences. I get to choose how my spending decisions force my hand with regard to my work. I can surround myself with people who generally make me feel good.

I am grateful for time. This one moment is what I know that I have. This very precious, unrepeatable, unpredictable second in time. How am I using it and what am I doing to experience it?

Precious Gifts

After my mother died, I received several personal notes from friends and clients. As I read them, I took a moment to mentally thank each writer for caring enough to send a condolence message. Most simply said that they held me and my family in their thoughts. And I know that as they took the minute or two to write that card, they really did hold us in their thoughts. That may be the most precious gift that any of us can give.

Don't worry about doing great things; do little things great. In these confusing and difficult times, I ask you to remember all that you have, and more important, all that you have to give.

SPEND YOUR LIFE WISELY.™

REPRINTED WITH PERMISSION BY THE FINANCIAL PLANNING ASSOCIATION, *Journal of Financial Planning*, DECEMBER 2008, ROSS LEVIN, "LIVING WITH GRACE."

For more information on the Financial Planning Association, please visit www.fpanet.org or call 1-800-322-4237.

Connections

When our daughters were little, we used to sing to them about the old lady that swallowed a fly. You might remember that she had to swallow a spider to eat the fly and a bird to eat the spider and so on. The lady died after swallowing a horse.

With my apologies to the composer, I have written some new lyrics for these times:

There Was an Economy That Depended on Oil

(To the tune of "There Was an Old Lady Who Swallowed a Fly")

There was an economy that depended on oil.
    I dunno why it depended on oil;
      perhaps it will spoil.
There was an economy that loved SUVs
    To haul all its workers far from the cities.
The cars pushed the economy
    to depend on more oil.
But I dunno why it depended on oil;
    perhaps it will spoil.

There was an economy with far away mansions
    That were easy to heat during economic
    expansions.
Folks commuted from mansions in those SUVs
    That hauled all those workers
    far from the cities.
The cars pushed the economy
    to depend on more oil.
But I dunno why it depended on oil;
    perhaps it will spoil.

There was an economy where people
    bought stuff
    Until all their creditors said,
    "That's enough."
They kept buying stuff to fill up the mansions;
They commuted from mansions in those SUVs
    That hauled all those workers
    far from the cities.
The cars pushed the economy to depend on
    more oil.
But I dunno why it depended on oil;
    perhaps it will spoil.

There was an economy where jobs
   were no more
   And those that existed were in Bangalore.
Folks borrowed and borrowed to buy all
   their stuff.
They kept buying stuff to fill up the mansions.
They commuted from mansions in those SUVs
   That hauled all those workers
   far from the cities.
The cars pushed the economy to depend on
   more oil.
But I dunno why it depended on oil;
   perhaps it will spoil.

There was an economy where interest
   rates rose;
It spoiled, I suppose.

Now, I don't think the economy is going to spoil. But I do think that things are far more connected than we had ever imagined. If you examine something like oil, you see that the rising cost of it and its sister, natural gas, means that people must dedicate more of their monthly cash flow to gasoline or heating bills. This leaves less money for things like going out to eat, or shopping, or vacations. Which means that restaurants, retail, and resorts might suffer. So, too, people like taxi drivers, waitresses, and dry cleaners, among a host of others. Which means there is less money to spend in the community. And on and on.

But oil represents an obvious connection. What about the more subtle connections that affect how we live? One thing that affects us is our abundance. While not everyone in the United States feels rich, compared with most of the world's people, we are doing pretty well.

In his book *A Whole New Mind*, about our move from the information to the conceptual age, Daniel Pink pointed out:

> "The United States spends more on trash bags than 90 other countries spend on everything. In other words, receptacles of our waste cost more than all of the goods consumed by nearly half of the world's nations."

Yet with all of this abundance, we are no happier as a nation than we were several decades ago. And perhaps no happier than some of those other 90 countries. And that, in part, is about connections. We talk about our need to simplify our lives as we see others around us complicating theirs. Yet the act of what others do has an influence over us. It works in good ways and not so good ways.

When someone does an incredible job of taking care of his or her yard, it makes us want to take care of ours. And when someone talks about their "gifted" kids—we must truly live in Lake Wobegon with all the parents talking about their above-average children—it is hard not to either feel bad or brag about our own. Sometimes these community connections push us. But they can also limit us.

So here is my proposal to begin within our community to connect to things more positively.

First, think about what tools you have to make a difference. You might be shocked at what you discover. Years ago I served on a volunteer board and I received a hand-written note from the chairman of the board thanking me for something that I said in the meeting. That had an enormous impact on me, and now I try to pass on as many handwritten notes as I can.

Second, think about doing something that you feel is right, just because it feels right. For a couple of years, our family has participated in the Xcel Energy Windsource program, which allows us to buy blocks of renewable energy equal to the energy used in our home. The program increases our energy bill, but such small acts by enough people can lead to very large changes.

Third, increase your giving. When money feels the scariest, you must do something to make it feel a little less important. I have always found that when I am feeling bad about money, if I give some of it up for others, it makes me feel a little better. And I know it's because in a small way I let money stop controlling me.

Fourth, try to look at what is going right with your life and focus on that. By thinking about what is working, you get to build off of your successes. Yes, there are always things that get in the way, but there is often far more that is right than we are willing to imagine.

SPEND YOUR LIFE WISELY.™

THIS COLUMN ORIGINALLY APPEARED IN THE MINNEAPOLIS *Star Tribune* ON OCTOBER 9, 2005.

3

Considering Family Matters and Money

Tolstoy opens *Anna Karenina* with "Happy families are all alike. Every unhappy family is unhappy in its own way." So while couples or family members may be quick to point out that money differences have caused all sorts of family problems, it is rarely the case. This may be the only time when it isn't about the money. Money issues are about control or love or attention.

This series of columns is about how to think about money within your family. Our goal as parents is to launch our children into the world; it is not to prevent them from experiencing struggle or heartache. Many of us think that by using our money to bail the kids out or prop them up, we are doing them a service. While that may be true in some instances, it is certainly not true as often as we would think.

The Art of Perception

My friend Phil was dating two women in college.

The women were in the same sorority, but each was unaware that Phil was involved with the other. He'd complain about how hard it was to juggle these relationships.

While many of us questioned the morality of Phil's choice, we couldn't help wishing that we had the same problems he had. That was until the women found out about each other through cross-referencing two ill-fated Valentine's personals placed in the *Minnesota Daily*. Suddenly, none of us wanted the problems that Phil had, and we all felt that he got what he deserved.

How often have we listened to others' perceived misery and thought, "I should have it so bad"? Consider the strong feelings about Paris Hilton's incarceration that surfaced across the nation.

I am not one to focus on the negative or to make excuses for millionaires behaving badly. But in financial planning, it is important to recognize that different people have different perceptions of their positions in life, and it is important to try to see things through their eyes.

Many of our clients come from inherited wealth. To an outside observer, it is easy to think that they have everything. While it is true that they may not have the same financial concerns as others, they still have a host of issues to confront.

First, one of the hardest things about money for most of us is that we have to make choices with it. We may not be able to buy the car that we want, live in the dream home, or even send our children to the schools that we want. But being forced to choose gives us context. It reinforces our values and helps us live life in a manner that's consistent with those values. When you have great wealth and don't have to make such choices, it is much harder to appreciate those things that you have.

Second, when we've worked for something, it reinforces our feelings of ownership. Saving for that first home at the expense of eating out or buying new clothes gives us that sense of ownership. When that home is bought for you, it takes away a rite of passage that can never be recaptured.

Third, we tend to hang out with people who are in similar situations to ours. We live in neighborhoods where most of us have similar levels of education and similar types of jobs. People who have inherited money are often in quite a different financial position than their social position. This can make inheritors feel isolated from their friends. Some even pretend that they don't have what they have. People with inherited wealth are often insecure about whether the people who know their financial situation associate with them because of their money. Are these people real friends or sycophants?

Finally, people with inherited wealth often have the conflicting feelings of entitlement and insecurity. Entitlement may come from growing up in an environment where they were waited on or got whatever financial thing they wanted. Insecurity may come from the fact that while not *having* enough was never an issue, not *being* enough was.

In the book *Bonds That Make Us Free*, C. Terry Warner wrote:

"Those times when we feel most miserable, offended, or angry are invariably the occasions when we're also most absorbed in ourselves and most anxious or suspicious or fearful, or in some other way concerned about ourselves."

Perhaps another way of looking at this is that in order for us to feel better, we need to create a self-justifying act, such as minimizing the importance of someone else's problems.

A friend was talking about how his daughter was trying to choose between a school that she wanted to go to and another school where she had won a scholarship. The trouble was that she was not excited about attending the school where she got the scholarship. The discussion between parent and child became quite heated around the expense of paying for the preferred school.

And while the parents focused on the money issue, their inability to listen to their child sprang more from their personal feelings around their own careers, successes, and a host of other factors. Their daughter never felt as though her position was really heard—and she was right.

I have learned in my job that trying to think about what I can do for someone rather than thinking about what I can get from them allows me to focus on what they are really saying. And when I succumb to thinking about how good someone has it, I hearken back to Phil's Valentine's Day massacre and realize things are not always as they seem.

SPEND YOUR LIFE WISELY.™
THIS COLUMN ORIGINALLY APPEARED IN THE MINNEAPOLIS *Star Tribune* ON JUNE 17, 2007.

The Value of Struggle

I made the mistake of finishing *The Kite Runner*, by Khaled Hosseini, the coming-of-age book set in Afghanistan during the revolution, at a coffee shop.

Having to discreetly bury my head and wipe my eyes while pledging never again to read a gut-wrenching book in a public place, I paged back to an early chapter that I think had an incredibly poignant financial planning moment.

A young Amir is playing cards with his friend and servant, Hassan. During their play, Amir grew ". . . sad for who Hassan was, where he lived. For how he'd accepted the fact that he would grow old in that mud shack in the yard, the way his father had." As Amir became lost in his thoughts, Hassan read his mind and said, "You know . . . I like where I live. It's my home."

Think about this. We often make our financial planning decisions based on assumptions. The assumptions go way beyond what rates of return we expect to earn or how long we plan to work. The assumptions also relate to what we think we want for ourselves and what we think others want. And these often-unspoken hopes are passed on from generation to generation. Some of these provide a framework from which good decisions can be made; others snag us in a net that catches our entire family. All of them have much more substance than we might think.

I was talking to a client about his children. He was saying that he wants to be sure his kids won't have to worry about money no matter what career they choose. The couple, therefore, wanted to set their children up with enough inheritance so that they could pursue their dreams.

Is that a noble goal? What parent wouldn't want the best for his or her children? The difficulty comes in determining what is best. Our initial assumption may be that we want to provide whatever we can for our children. But let's look at this assumption on several levels.

First, do we really want to eliminate all struggles from our children's lives? If you cut a butterfly out of its chrysalis before it fights its way out, it will die. The struggle is necessary for the caterpillar to go through its metamorphosis.

In life, our struggles often form the basis of our stories and our success. They are what can help define us. We want to help our children through their struggles, but we don't want to eliminate the struggles.

When deciding how—or whether—to pay for college, for example, don't automatically assume that taking care of everything is best. Maybe your children should work for their spending money or for a sizable percentage of their school costs. It is appropriate for parents to save for college, but don't feel compelled to pay for it all. If you build up savings, this gives you the flexibility to work with your child on an appropriate division of costs.

Second, can we safely assume that our children will be more comfortable with our money? Money can be stratifying. For example, if your children want to enter a life of service in which they won't earn much, they most likely will be with a peer group that has similar societal aims and earnings ceilings. This means that any money you have given your kids could automatically isolate them from their friends. Financially, they will be able to take different trips, drive different cars, and live in different homes than many others in their field.

If they are uncomfortable with this, they may choose to pretend they don't have money so they can feel more similar to their friends. Our inherited-wealth clients who have been the most comfortable with their finances tend to be those who have had a history of open communication with their parents about money and who have received their inheritance without strings.

Third, do we want to deprive our children of the experiences that gave our lives context? Yes, having money can cause deprivation. If you remember what it was like to save for your first car or your first home, you can relate to how it felt when you actually made the purchase. Sure, the home probably was pretty small, in desperate need of paint, and was not in the exact neighborhood in which you hoped to live, but it was yours.

Contrast that with giving the keys to your dream home to your children. While it may seem the right thing to do, don't make that decision for them.

Fourth, are we assuming that we are really doing this for our children, or are we doing it for ourselves? It

82

may be a tough pill to swallow, but you need to think about whether you are trying to replace yourself with your money. Are you doing these things for your kids because you feel it is the right thing to do, or are you doing them because you weren't around enough and need to assuage your guilt? Or because your neighbors just did it for their kids? Or because you didn't have these luxuries growing up?

Fifth, will your kids assume that you feel that they are incompetent? This may be a message that you are unintentionally sending. Sometimes in families, one child may do well financially while another struggles. We want to help the child we feel has been short-changed. But should we? This answer depends on the dynamics of the whole family and needs to be discussed with everyone involved.

We tend to see the world through our own lenses. We automatically think that our children want what we want. Not only is this often not the case, but our kids often cannot bring themselves to tell us.

What are the assumptions around money with which you conduct your life? Do they accurately portray your hopes, dreams, and values? And are you inclusive with

your family and willing to validate these assumptions with them?

Whether you intend it or not, your children look to you for clues to what you want for them. Don't you think you should talk with them about what they want for themselves?

SPEND YOUR LIFE WISELY.™
THIS COLUMN ORIGINALLY APPEARED IN THE MINNEAPOLIS *Star Tribune* ON JANUARY 16, 2005.

Gains and Losses

I did something really stupid. I sold our cabin.

It wasn't just my decision. But I planted the seed in my wife's mind a few years ago.

"We really aren't using it that much. The kids are in activities. There are so many places that we want to visit. It has appreciated so nicely. We could sell it and invest all the proceeds."

Finally, my wife agreed to let realtors look at it. Right away one of them wanted to do a one-time showing. We agreed, with the stipulation that we would not negotiate on price or terms. To our amazement, the cabin sold. This was a Thursday. On Sunday, my wife informed me, "We can't sell the cabin." Panicked, I told her that it was a done deal. We couldn't back out. We had a binding agreement.

So we sold our cabin. But my image of investing the proceeds and using them for vacations whenever we wanted

to go also disappeared with the cabin sale. We hadn't actually sold a cabin; we'd sold memories of the girls in their rain boots catching frogs on the banks of the lake. We'd sold the cry of the loons singing us to sleep. We'd sold mosquito-filled Fourth of Julys and deer watching at night.

No matter how I tried to justify it, buying a bunch of pharmaceutical stocks did not measure up to picking a basket of wild raspberries or blueberries. I'd blown it.

But after reading a book by a Harvard psychology professor, Daniel Gilbert, *Stumbling on Happiness*, at least I better understand the error of my ways.

We often don't realize that "we make different comparisons at different times." I was viewing the sale of our cabin as a potential gain—"I can't wait to invest this money!" My wife was looking at it as a potential loss— "We won't have our family getaway anymore!"

On the other hand, once the cabin was sold, another strange thing occurred. "The kinds of comparisons we are naturally making as buyers and sellers are not the kinds of comparisons we will naturally make once we become owners and former owners," Gilbert says.

As former owners, we began to look at the things that had needed repairing around the cabin and the work involved. We talked about how we had always wished it had been a year-round place, and how we had never loved the location. In other words, our psychological immune systems kicked in. Gilbert says this "defends the mind against unhappiness in much the same way that the physical immune system defends the body against illness."

We began to look at how the mistake/decision occurred and what we could do to try to repair the damage. We knew that things would not be the same, but we knew that there were other things we could do that could make things even better.

We took the girls to the conference room of my office on a Saturday. With big white sheets of paper and colored markers, each of us drew our own interconnected webs of ideas related to how we would define a "family vacation property."

The formal term for this exercise is mind-mapping, a form of brainstorming. Each of us drew a picture of a vacation property in the center of the paper and made lines extending from it with words or ideas that the picture generated. Some of these words would create new ideas or visions from which further lines were drawn. When we were finished, we shared what we had written and drawn.

The exercise led us to dream about our next step. It was interesting that most of our concepts had little in common with the cabin we sold. I would suggest this is because of Gilbert's idea of "habituation." We had already become accustomed to the features of our old cabin, so when we were thinking about a family vacation property, we were looking at things with fresh eyes.

Armed with our mind maps, we set out to look for a new cabin. I was completely on board with the prospect of doing something different. Because of a great realtor, we found a place that pretty much matched the images we had created. And it is year-round, on a small lake in an area that is a wonderful combination of privacy and activity.

We closed on it Monday.

Stumbling on Happiness points out how difficult it is for any of us to try to predict the future. We base our guesses on where we are today, but every new experience changes our perspective.

I never would have predicted that I would own a cabin a month after I sold one. But being the holistic financial planner that I am, I never would have thought I could make such a one-dimensional decision to begin with.

SPEND YOUR LIFE WISELY.™
THIS COLUMN ORIGINALLY APPEARED IN THE MINNEAPOLIS *Star Tribune* ON AUGUST 20, 2006.

Real Retirement

One of our 50-something clients e-mailed me after having a frustrating day on the road. He wanted to know when he could retire. I responded that I don't want him to quit work, because he will spend his days sitting in our lobby, drinking our coffee, and chatting me up.

He e-mailed back that our coffee is bad and my company is worse. That was unfair. We happen to serve very good coffee.

This economy has some people thinking about retirement. The reduction in workforce is forcing employees to work longer hours, often for less pay. Early retirement packages have been offered to some who want it and, unfortunately, to many who had no choice. Some people feel the drop in their portfolios may force them to work forever. Over the years, we have worked with a number of retirees, and I want to share with you some observations of those who have retired successfully.

First, retirement expectations should be grounded in previous patterns of behavior. Couples who spent a lot of time together while working often enjoy their time together in retirement. But there are many situations where one partner spent long hours in a job, while the other partner took care of everything else. The excited new retiree suddenly finds himself or herself encroaching upon sacred space. "For better or worse, but not for lunch," is more than a cute punch line. Developing a plan for each partner individually, in addition to as a couple, is a critical first step in preparing for retirement.

Find an outlet for your energy. One of our clients is trying to understand what this transition will look like. While he has the financial wherewithal to walk away from a career, he has always focused intensely on his field. Before he retires completely, he may need to either develop some different work habits in a new, potentially part-time role or develop something outside of work to which he can dedicate his intensity. This work personality trait follows the physics law of the conservation of energy—it remains constant over time. So unless something meaningful can substitute for work, this energy will now focus on his partner's spending or what's wrong with the kids.

Man or woman at work is completely different than money at work. People who have done the best job of saving are usually the worst at living off of their assets. The act of saving is an act of deprivation—you are putting off for tomorrow what you could do today.

But you need to spend those assets at some point. Some people combat this by investing in bond ladders and only living off of interest. This strategy works best for those who have low spending requirements relative to their portfolio size and no need to keep pace with inflation. Unfortunately, everyone else must own some stocks and create a spending model based on a percentage of the portfolio, rather than simply the income from the portfolio.

If implemented appropriately, you have a better chance of holding spending relatively constant with this approach (even though your portfolio may move around) than with an all-bond portfolio. For example, if you set up a 10-year Treasury bond ladder, your Treasury that was paying over 5.5 percent a decade ago now pays 3.5 percent. That represents a 36 percent drop in spending—without considering inflation.

Get comfortable with uncertainty and change. The changes that occur in and around retirement are startling. Parents and friends pass away and grandchildren are born. Dexterity is lost. During the early years of retirement, we encourage our clients to use their resources for experiences. Change is gradual until it isn't. One of our clients is dealing with end-of-life issues with his spouse. She now lives in a full-time care facility. When he comes in and talks about her, he recalls the times they spent together traveling, going out to dinner, and taking walks. Pleasant memories expand—be sure to create them.

One way to handle change is to memorialize your life through a professional video. An interviewer asks questions about your life stories. This can be a fantastic way to provide a permanent legacy that lives on far beyond you.

And take some time to prepare for your death. In his book, *Chasing Daylight—How My Forthcoming Death*

Transformed My Life, Eugene O'Kelly writes, "If how we die is one of the most important decisions we can make . . . then why do most people abrogate this responsibility?"

There is much to plan around the celebration of what was your life. Take the time to do it rather then wasting it away drinking bad coffee.

SPEND YOUR LIFE WISELY.™

THIS COLUMN ORIGINALLY APPEARED IN THE MINNEAPOLIS *Star Tribune* ON NOVEMBER 22, 2009.

What's Your Legacy?

A couple of years ago, I took one of my daughters to the Simpson House Annual Homeless March and Vigil, an event honoring the homeless men, women, and children who have died that year in Minnesota.

As we sat through the service, I realized we were surrounded by people whose faces I had avoided while stopped at a red light or glimpsed while driving under a freeway overpass. Each had a name and a story. Some of their friends stood up and talked about how they had shared stories together and how the deceased had made them feel special. Others stood up and commended them for their military service. All of those honored had made names for themselves.

My daughter and I left feeling moved, troubled, and yet somehow happy that we could recognize these people in our community.

When we think about the impact of money, we seem to focus on the day-to-day. We wonder whether we are spending too much or making too little. But what if we spent some real time thinking about who we want to be and how we will be remembered. Every day we are creating memories for those around us.

What are some steps that we can take in our financial plan to try to leave a lasting impact?

The first step is to not run away from the money issues. Family discussions about money are often uncomfortable, but they are important. Attempting to understand and explain your money attitudes in regular family meetings brings a tremendous amount of clarity to the family—and to you.

For example, if you have decided to pay for your children's college education, have you thought about and discussed why you want to pay? Is it because you want them to be able to focus on their education so that they can get good grades and do post-graduate work? Is it because your college was paid for and you see where it got you? Is it because your college wasn't paid for and you remember how hard it was?

As a business owner, I am always attracted to the résumés of people who had to work through college because

I know that they understand the value of work, budgeting, and sacrifice. Do I want to raise children whose résumés I would throw in the "maybe" pile if they were interviewing with me?

There is not one right answer, only right questions. But the questions and discussions determine who you are going to be.

The second step is to not use your money as a means of control, but rather as one of your many resources. Control comes in many forms. Direct control used properly is a valuable tool. Paying people for performing well in their jobs is a positive example of this. But using it in your family to pay for behavior is destructive. We have seen clients use their wills as a form of punishment when family therapy may have been a better alternative. We have seen children act in accordance with their parents' wishes at the expense of their own life dreams.

Sometimes the control is unintentional. We have seen the best-intentioned parents try to pass on their family cabins. While there are certain instances where this works beautifully, we have seen a number of times where this has not worked at all. Each of your children has different circumstances. Many times the kids feel awkward letting you know that they love the cabin but won't want it after you're gone. Most times, one child wants it while the others are less certain. But even the child who wants to keep the cabin may not want it if it is his or her sole inheritance—or if he or she has to buy out siblings.

Before you tell your kids how you want them to handle this, please remember that you will no longer be around to enforce your choice. If you wish to have your legacy be about control, then trying to rule from the grave is a terrific way to ensure it.

The third step in making your name is to act in accordance with your values, not simply prescribe those values. Through almost 25 years of financial planning, what has become clear to me is that children usually follow in the financial footsteps of their parents (although some try to veer as far off the path as possible). Parents who are afraid of their money raise money-scared children. Philanthropic parents seem to breed children who want to make a difference.

As always, it is how we act, not what we say. And the actions relate to all that we do. Author Karen Casey says:

"Seemingly insignificant relationships are as important as very memorable ones. Believing this will change every experience in one's life."

This year at the homeless vigil (details at simpsonhousing.org), we will again be sitting with people who have made names for themselves, although maybe not the names they had thought they would make. What shall we say about you?

SPEND YOUR LIFE WISELY.™
THIS COLUMN ORIGINALLY APPEARED IN THE MINNEAPOLIS *Star Tribune* ON DECEMBER 17, 2006.

4

Exploring Business and Financial Styles

None of us sees things in the same way. Each of us is bombarded with information and messages that we then interpret and upon which we finally act. There is an entire field called behavioral finance that deals with the seeming disconnect between what completely "rational" people would do and the weird decisions we all make.

Yet for some reason, we are supposed to believe that, regardless of our differences, one size fits all. You should spend your money in a certain way, invest in a particular manner, and divide your estate according to fundamental principles. But this is not the case. Good financial planning takes into consideration not only your values, but your idiosyncrasies as well to make sure that your financial plan is effective and personal.

Money Style

I have a deal with my 11-year-old daughters. They receive an allowance of $11 a week. My wife and I expect that they put some of that into our "giving jar" to be donated to a charity of their choice. For every dollar they give us to put in the bank to be held for a year, we match it. They therefore get 100 percent return on their savings. (After all, it's only fair that my daughters get the same return as my clients.)

Anyway, their bank statements came yesterday. One of my daughters, who is sort of a spendthrift, has already accumulated $150 in her savings account, but she's spent all the rest of her money. The other daughter has only $50 in the savings account. The one with the least amount of money in the account, though, has $150 in cash that she has saved to buy an iPod. So (when you deduct my match), daughter 1 has saved $75 and daughter 2, $175. It is evident that the iPod daughter is putting away more money each month, but it is being invested for future consumption, not growth.

As I thought about this, I realized what great financial planning lessons I am learning from my girls. Each of them is doing something very different from the other, yet they are both experiencing the most basic core financial planning skills.

Daughter 1 (I am purposely not naming them so that they don't get pigeonholed by their preadolescent behavior) sees something and wants it. Her way to gain discipline is to hand over a portion of her allowance the second it touches her hands, so that she won't have a chance to spend it. This has led to a large bank account and also a large stash of cheap knick-knacks that she enjoys. In practice, she is paying herself first.

Daughter 2 is directing her savings for a purpose. She has made a conscious decision that she wants the iPod this year, so she can't meet the requirement of banking the money and watching it double. She has also decided exactly what she wants, so she doesn't cavalierly spend her allowance on sweets or toys. This is in line with the simple fact of money—its purpose is to ultimately spend or distribute.

What's interesting is my reaction. I am way more comfortable with what daughter 2 is doing. Even though less is going into the bank, I don't see her "wasting" as much on stuff that is not important to her. My wife has helped me in not making comments about my value system when they are so diligently following theirs. Both children are making financial planning decisions that are appropriate for where they are and what they want.

When I ascribe my judgments to what my daughters are doing with their money, I am trying to steer them toward my philosophies of money. But my money "stuff" is as messed up as anyone's. I hate spending money. I love to invest it and watch it grow. I hate having stuff. To me, stuff is just something to break or to covet. And yet, somewhat paradoxically, I also love nice things. I love experiences. And I love stuff that matters to me. (I mean, how many pairs of running shorts does someone really need? Oh my gosh—I am daughter 1!!)

Understand Their Money Styles
So what is our role with our clients? We have to try to understand what their money styles are and work within those parameters. My daughters have different money styles and are each making authentic decisions based on them. My clients have different money styles, but are their decisions consistent with those styles? Many of our clients are partnered where one is like daughter 1 and

the other like daughter 2. I need to be careful to not side with whomever is most like me. I need to be able to stay connected to them and assist working through what essential compromises need to take place so that they are both fulfilled. But the only way to do that is to recognize that my personal money view is my own. It is not right for everyone (and at times, it may not even be right for me).

We sure preach a lot in this business. I think it is good to know what you stand for and to express it. But I also think it is good to recognize that what you espouse is an opinion—one that is important to you, but one that is yours. And no matter how smart you are, your opinions have been carved out of your own life experiences. Make sure that there is also room for others who have had their own experiences.

SPEND YOUR LIFE WISELY.™

REPRINTED WITH PERMISSION BY THE FINANCIAL PLANNING ASSOCIATION, *Journal of Financial Planning*, JULY 2004, ROSS LEVIN, "MAKE ROOM FOR OTHERS' EXPERIENCES."

For more information on the Financial Planning Association, please visit www.fpanet.org or call 1-800-322-4237.

Delusions

I read the cover story in my February *Runner's World* magazine about an ultra-marathoner. His goal is to run 300 miles without stopping. The story went on to talk about how he runs more than 100 miles a week, cross-trains by taking a few hours weekly to go wind surfing, puts in 60 hours a week running his own company, and advises, "Don't be selfish." He schedules his twice-monthly, 75-plus mile runs at 2 a.m. when the kids are tucked in bed. "Nighttime runs leave me more time to be with my family," he says.

Now, I often find this magazine inspiring, but as I was reading this article I was beginning to feel bad about myself. I mean, I could barely haul my sorry butt out of bed to go to work the morning after watching the Oscars, and this guy is running the equivalent of Minneapolis to Hinckley in the middle of the night!

I began to come up with a number of words to describe him, such as dedicated, disciplined, determined. And then I struck on maybe the most fitting one—delusional.

This marathon man is spending at least 80 hours a week between work and exercise, and he says, "Don't be selfish."

Hello? Anyone home? Rather than feeling bad about myself, I realized that not only do I not want what he has, but I am pretty content with most of my own choices.

I started thinking about how often we take for granted what others say and how we allow that to influence us— and how often what we hear are delusions. For example, remember when Lasik eye surgery was just becoming the thing? And when brokerage firms came out with projections on how the growth rate for the machines for the procedure was going to explode?

The message was as clear as your post-surgery eyesight—buy the company that made those machines, no matter how expensive it was. That turned out to be an optical delusion. None of the projections came close to coming true, and the stock totally fell out of bed. But if you talked to anyone who owned that stock early on and listened to how rich they were becoming, you felt bad about your own investments.

Every day I hear more of these delusions. Here are some of my favorites, and here is how to change your thinking around them:

"I'm not greedy, I just want a 10 percent rate of return." This is a pretty common one. In fact, you may be thinking this yourself. Here is what is wrong with this thinking: We currently are in an environment where 10-year Treasury bonds are paying a little less than 4.5 percent. So if you have 80 percent of your portfolio in stocks and 20 percent in bonds, stocks would need to earn almost 11.5 percent to get you to that magical 10 percent.

But over long periods of time, stocks consistently have performed at a rate of about 7 percent above inflation (real rate of return). So unless inflation comes screaming back or we return to the statistically outlying market of the 1990s, a consistent portfolio return of 10 percent probably will be elusive. And yet you will hear investment managers throw that number out as though it means something. And here is the bigger issue: If inflation is low, you need a lower rate of return to stay ahead of it. I think inflation is going to creep, not roar, back.

So diversify your investments, ignore the myths of investment success at cocktail parties, save an appropriate percentage of your income, and set aside thoughts of 10 percent returns along with your eyeglasses after successful laser surgery.

"I can't wait to slow down when I retire." This is a favorite of mine. People who spend all their time either at the office or thinking about work believe that retirement will be an event whereby they suddenly will be able to relax. There is a description for this kind of idea—delusional. Danish philosopher Søren Kierkegaard said that "Life can only be understood backwards; but it must be lived forward."

Many years of working with clients has shown me a pretty consistent pattern—those who have been compulsive with their work need to be compulsive with a hobby in order to be able to retire, and those who lived a pretty balanced life are going to have a pretty balanced retirement. Either slow down now or be prepared to be gunning it all the way to your end.

"I can't afford to give more to charity." This may touch a nerve, but most people who say this are deluding themselves. It generally has been my experience that when you are intentional with your philanthropy, several things happen. First, your money doesn't become as important to you because you are not spending it all on yourself. Second, your actions are helping to serve others who in their own turn will help others. Third, you will appreciate all that you have.

"I don't have time to plan." This one is delusional because a more accurate statement would be, "I choose to spend my time doing other things than plan for the future that I hope to have."

That doesn't sound nearly as glamorous as being too busy. In the book *Siddhartha*, by Hermann Hesse, as the protagonist is in the middle of searching for his spiritual awakening, he says:

> "The reason why I do not know anything about myself . . . is due to one thing. . . . I was afraid of myself, I was fleeing from myself."

This may be the biggest reason people choose not to plan. They are afraid of what they may discover about either themselves or their abilities to do what they feel they want. But the amazing thing about planning is that it is liberating, not confining. A plan gives you clear boundaries, which give you limits. And it is within these limits that opportunities exist.

Sometimes it can be hard to face the truth, but not facing it is worse than a 75-mile run in the middle of the night.

SPEND YOUR LIFE WISELY.™
THIS COLUMN ORIGINALLY APPEARED IN THE MINNEAPOLIS *Star Tribune* ON MARCH 13, 2005.

True Self

On a recent trip, I finished reading James Stewart's somewhat horrifying book, *Disney War*. It outlined in graphic detail the inner workings of the business of Disney and, more alarmingly, the politics of Disney. And it showed what a brilliant and horribly flawed leader Michael Eisner was.

I finished that book and took a shower. I needed to cleanse myself of the awful hubris about which I had read. Courtesy of some major business scandals and tremendous business books about them, I am the cleanest I have ever been. My shower is in constant use, my hair shines, and my teeth sparkle. Unfortunately, there seems to be an inverse relationship between what is good for society and my personal hygiene.

I have read scores of business books. What I am realizing as I read them is that even the people whom we felt were the most gifted business leaders often were either only good at one thing, or were lucky to get one thing right, or were just in the right place at the right time. Yet we want to sit at their knees and learn lessons from the masters. Here is the nasty little secret: There are no business masters and everyone is a business master. More importantly, each of us has our own internal mastery of something.

Business Lessons from Nonbusiness Books

So on this trip I read some other books that I think provide far better business lessons. Let me share some of my favorite quotes from them:

The Sermon on the Mount, by Emmet Fox:

> "[O]ur lives are just the result of the kind of thoughts we have chosen to hold; and therefore they are of our own ordering. . ."

When we think about what we want to do to grow our business, maybe it is better to think about what we want to do to serve our clients. I can't think of a better industry where your success is more closely linked with that of your clients. And as we continue to explore ways to make their lives better, ours will surely follow.

The Heart of Buddha's Teaching, by Thich Nhat Hanh:

> "[I]t is often our very idea of happiness that prevents us from being happy."

If only I had a billion dollars under management . . . if only I could work with Mrs. Jones . . . if only my wife would appreciate how hard this career is . . . Instead of waiting for the next thing to happen, take an inventory of all that you have to appreciate in this very moment. Then see which actions in your life do not match those of the Eightfold Path (Right View, Right Thinking, Right Speech, Right Action, Right Livelihood, Right Diligence, Right Mindfulness, and Right Concentration) and how those actions prevent you from living your authentic life.

The Four Agreements, by Don Miguel Ruiz:

> "(1) Be impeccable with your word; (2) Don't take anything personally; (3) Don't make assumptions; (4) Always do your best."

I can't even begin to think of all the times I have received a phone message and worried about what I might have missed. Or how often someone might say something to me that I end up ruminating over instead of really listening to what they had said. Or how seriously someone else might take a throw-away comment by me. These simple "agreements" have already saved me significant consternation.

The Power of Now, by Eckhart Tolle:

> "Stress is caused by being 'here' but wanting to be 'there,' or being in the present but wanting to be in the future."

We can get so far ahead of ourselves in thinking about what really matters. If we could focus instead on the immediate task at hand, we actually would be doing what matters.

What We Do, Who We Are
While I can't say I enjoyed each of these books, I can say I learned something from each. And one of the things they reinforced is that we cannot separate what we do from who we are. The decisions we make for our businesses are reflections of what we value. Those value decisions may be made unconsciously, but they are being made.

At Accredited Investors, we are constantly making decisions as our company grows. We have 25 people and $450 million that we manage for clients, so it seems that the stakes of our choices are very high. But they are no more or less than what you face with your practice. And I know that whether we are right or wrong about the decisions we make as a company, they are not as much about *foresight* as they are about *insight*. It is presumptuous for us to think that we can forecast the direction of the future. The future will happen whether we want it to or not. But we can make decisions that maximize the present.

Whom you partner with, whom you hire, and whom you choose for clients are statements about who you are at that moment. And who you are in the present will tell you something about who you will ultimately be. But to get these decisions right, you need to take the time to develop your core values. You need to ask *how* will you serve before asking *whom* will you serve. Why you are in business should be understood before you consider how big you want your business to be.

I completely failed to predict what our business would look like. I thought we would stay much smaller than we are. I thought my personal freedoms would decrease as we got bigger instead of increase. And I thought our clients would work only with me instead of them finding great people within our firm with whom they are comfortable working. But none of that really mattered because the question that we always were asking was: "What is right for right now?" And when we actually listened, we made good decisions. And when we didn't, we didn't.

What is right for you right now? You are already grown up, so don't be thinking about what you want to be when you grow up. What do you want to be right now?

SPEND YOUR LIFE WISELY.™

REPRINTED WITH PERMISSION BY THE FINANCIAL PLANNING ASSOCIATION, *Journal of Financial Planning*, JULY 2005, ROSS LEVIN, "TAPPING INTO YOUR OWN BRILLIANCE."

For more information on the Financial Planning Association, please visit www.fpanet.org or call 1-800-322-4237.

5

Making Sound Financial Decisions

With the benefit of hindsight, we would all know where we should invest, what we should avoid, how much to save, and to what extent we can freely enjoy our money. But when we are enmeshed in life, we are making decisions with incomplete information.

There can be a big difference between making good decisions and having good results, or making bad decisions yet experiencing good results. People who made money in tech stocks, or real estate, or any other bubble, experienced good results until their bad decisions came home to roost. And those who avoided those extravagances probably felt awful about their good, but temporarily unfruitful, decisions. Developing a plan comes from first looking at the why before you spend a second of time on the how. Creating flexibility for the implementation of the how is the foundation for sound decision making.

Too Bad to Be True

Monday, March 9, was the day that I can point to when fear ran wild. Headlines screamed at us: "Unemployment rises to 8.1 percent!" "The world confronts its first global recession since World War II!" The stock market responded by falling to its 12-year low.

I was talking to a friend, an executive at a large mutual fund company, who said that the company call center's volume of people desperately trying to sell their stocks reached a fever pitch. Maybe you were one of those who rushed to the exits.

But a funny thing happened the next day. The market started to climb back. Some people who sold on Monday wanted back in on Wednesday. The very same emotions that drove them from a market they feared was going to zero were now making them fear they had just missed the rebound. Neither of those scenarios was real.

One thing is real: Things are too bad to be true.

Ponzi schemes such as those of Bernie Madoff or Stanford Financial obviously were too good to be true. The economy is the opposite—things are simply too bad to be true. While things are difficult and will get worse, they will not stay that way.

In his book *The Next 100 Years—A Forecast for the 21st Century*, George Friedman, a renowned expert in geopolitics and forecasting, wrote:

> "American culture is the manic combination of exultant hubris and profound gloom."

He pointed out that in the 1950s, one of the most popular books in this country was *The Age of Anxiety*. Fifty years after the success of that book, we predictably find ourselves with similar anxiety for different reasons.

We know that there will continue to be a string of bank failures, but they won't be anything like the thousands per week that we saw during the Depression. We know that unemployment is rising, but according to some reports, 60 percent of the workforce thinks their jobs are in danger. We know that our deficit is going to grow, but it has grown (and shrunk) before. Doom is predicted, and it is too bad to be true.

Friedman wrote:

> "When it comes to the future, the only thing one can be sure of is that common sense will be wrong. . . . The things that appear to be so permanent and dominant at any given moment in history can change with stunning rapidity."

So while common sense may have told you to sell everything on March 9, there are better ways of looking at things.

Time Horizon

We don't know whether we are in the middle of a bear market rally or the next bull market, but we do know that things never go straight up or straight down. While it is very tempting to try to time this market, the way to do so is not by being completely in or totally out. The plan you need to develop must match your time horizon and your ultimate use of the money.

Your time horizon is determined by when you are going to spend your money—not by your age. People in their 70s or 80s who intend to leave their portfolio to children or charity have a longer time horizon than those who know that they are going to buy a house in the next couple of years.

If you have been investing in stocks, and because of either disposition or needs you should have simply been saving in the bank, your strategy should be to sell equities and raise cash during these market rallies until you reach the cash position with which you are comfortable. Keep peeling money away when the market rises to predetermined levels, and set two to three of these levels.

If you panicked and sold stocks when you should have stayed invested, you need to decide first whether you are the type of investor who is able to cope with the volatility that goes hand-in-hand with long-term stock market returns. If you can be a long-term investor, then look at putting money to work when the market falls to predetermined levels. Invest some now and put more in when the market drops until you reach a place where you are fully invested. And diversify—large, small, and international stocks still make sense. Currently, we are emphasizing large stocks, but we still have holdings in other areas.

There will continue to be bad news that may cause markets to move dramatically down; if the news is less bad than expected, the markets will move dramatically up. In spite of the volatility, if your investment plan matches your financial plan, you can take solace in the notion that things are too bad to be true.

SPEND YOUR LIFE WISELY.™

THIS COLUMN ORIGINALLY APPEARED IN THE MINNEAPOLIS *Star Tribune* ON MARCH 22, 2009.

Choices

Comedian Steven Wright said, "You can't have everything. Where would you put it?" But the wisdom of that quote often gets lost in our day-to-day living. The ability to choose is one of the basic tenets of American society. It is an incredibly powerful freedom that most of us would not consider giving up. But all too often we forget the touchstone of this freedom: actually choosing. Not only can we not have everything, but if we exhibit lack of discipline by going after things that we have no business wanting, I believe that we risk losing what's important.

In a world of limitless options, the abundance of choices can leave us unfulfilled. By refusing to narrow our choices, we may seem to be staying nimble, but we are really giving up the gift of appreciating what we have. Harvard Divinity Professor Peter Gomes, in his book The Good Life, says:

> "[T]he freedom to get and to do and to have [is] insufficient in comparison with the freedom to

be." He goes on to say that we should "use that freedom so that we do not become slaves to what freedom allows us to obtain."

We have a responsibility to be responsible. And in our interconnected world, it is critical that this responsibility transcends our homes and extends into our communities and even those places that we may never actually visit.

In our financial world, all of our choices have ripple effects that often go beyond money. Sure, stretching for the new house means increased costs for insurance, property taxes, and utilities, not to mention upgrading the furniture. But it may also mean that we are in a new neighborhood with people who have more money than we do and therefore our family is influenced by the externalities imposed by our neighbors' values. It could mean that the schools our children attend have a different type of pressure to which our kids must adjust. It may mean that our drive to work is longer (or shorter), availing us of either more or less time at home. And it may make us feel that we can no longer take career risks because we have adapted to our surroundings and the stakes of potentially giving them up have now become too high.

Although we may actually seek some of these results, others may cause unexpected collateral damage.

So it is important to be aware of what we are choosing. And it is important to understand how we choose. In his book, *The Paradox of Choice*, Swarthmore College Prof. Barry Schwartz theorizes:

> "[A] large array of options may diminish the attractiveness of what people actually choose. The reason being that thinking about the attractions of some of the unchosen options detracts from the pleasure derived from the chosen one."

Schwartz basically thinks that there are two types of ways people make decisions. Maximizers are people who must feel certain that every decision they make is the absolute best. They require a tremendous amount of information and must understand what all the alternatives are before they are willing to make a choice. Satisficers are those people who are comfortable with choices that are good enough. It doesn't matter that there are better opportunities if the one that they have chosen can make them comfortable.

Most of us probably lean in one direction or the other, but could fall in either camp depending on the choice.

Schwartz's research has shown that people who are maximizers tend to be less happy than satisficers. Maximizers ruminate more about their decisions, are often confronted with new information later that may make them regret their choice and have seen so many alternatives that their final selection would never fully integrate all the positive aspects of each of the options they reviewed.

Choosing Styles

In your financial planning, there are a couple of areas where you should be a maximizer and a host of others where satisficing would do. Maximizing is most important throughout the qualitative phase of planning. The most important thing you can work on is your goal setting. This is where you are determining what matters most in your life. You are making the value judgments about your career, your family, your time, and your integrity. These are areas that cannot be compromised and need to be fully developed before entering the quantitative aspect of planning.

For most of the quantitative segment, you should be satisficing. For example, in investment planning, asset allocation is the ultimate in satisficing. By choosing to be in a variety of investment classes, you are choosing to achieve more consistent returns over time. You are sacrificing being solely invested in the best investment class in any year. But you are also eliminating the chance of being solely in the worst investment class as well. Think about the emotional anguish that you will save. I believe that by satisficing through asset allocation, you are actually maximizing both the psychological and actual return on investment.

If you don't want to work with a professional for your investment choices, you still can choose a satisficing approach by buying index funds to fulfill each asset class.

Insurance planning is another area where you can probably be OK by satisficing. While there are dramatic differences between insurance companies for whole life policies, this is not necessarily the case for term life. Once you have decided how much term life insurance you need, you may be able to meet this need by performing a simple Google search for "low-cost term insurance." If you choose to buy from a company with a high rating, you most likely will be well-served.

You can also satisfice on your mortgage. Rates are changing all the time. When you lock in a rate with which you are comfortable, just check it a couple of times a year to see whether it makes sense to refinance. The cost of trying to catch the bottom of the mortgage market is probably higher than refinancing when you are comfortable with the new rate.

Get over the thought that there is one best way to solve your financial questions. There are often many acceptable roads to take. Trust your instincts and do what you feel is right, and you will probably be better off than sifting through endless reams of conflicting and tantalizing data.

SPEND YOUR LIFE WISELY.™
THIS COLUMN ORIGINALLY APPEARED IN THE MINNEAPOLIS *Star Tribune* ON SEPTEMBER 12, 2004.

In the Moment

I love to watch birds. When I go on walks in the morning with our dogs, I try to appreciate all the sounds of the dawn songbirds just getting their start on the day. I really got a chance to appreciate birds over the Memorial Day weekend.

We went up north with some friends and their kids. One of the fathers, Dave, is an avid birder. He can identify virtually any species of bird by its song. He knows whether to look up or down, to the swamp or the forest or the ground. He can see something winging overhead and know immediately what it is. And he can detect subtleties in the birds that my untrained eye can't notice.

Since my hearing is no longer perfect and my eyesight is getting worse, I spent a considerable amount of my time anxiously waiting for direction from Dave. But as we walked and listened and looked, I was thinking about how my experience with birds is not very different from our experiences with money.

Know where you are

To be a good birder, you must understand something about the birds. You must know what birds you would expect to find in a particular habitat so that you have a better chance of identifying them in the twinkling you might have to see them.

With money, so much of our angst comes from not really understanding where we are. Sure, we might have a sense of what assets we have or what debts we owe. We might even be fairly clear on what we spend. But those items are secondary to the understanding of what is driving us.

Are we working or saving to try to build a better life for ourselves or to build a life that we think we should want? Have we taken an inventory with our partners to determine what is driving each of us?

Take some time to reflect on what has worked for you in the past with money. Think about when you really felt that you were making decisions that were consistent with your values, not your fears.

I suspect that when you think about this, you won't necessarily be focusing on items but rather on experiences. In

Emerson, The Mind on Fire, author Robert Richardson quotes Ralph Waldo Emerson as saying, "No man has learned anything until he knows that every day is Judgment Day."

Every day is our chance to get a sense of where we are and to listen to the feelings we have when we know that something is not right. Acting on those feelings is probably your most important financial step.

Someone Who's Been There

I learned more in two hours looking for birds with Dave than I had in my countless hours of going through bird books or trying to distinguish calls from a bird CD. Dave taught me patterns and shortcuts that I could not have learned on my own. He could see little variations in species that would have been almost impossible for me to see by myself.

The great thing about money is that there is no shortage of advice. The problem with money is that there is no shortage of advice.

Who do you know who is doing money right? Think about two or three people who seem to be in a financial situation similar to yours but who have more of what you want. Maybe they create more family time. Maybe they travel more. Maybe they seem to be comfortable with what they have. Talk to them. Look to these mentors even before you talk to a professional. They might give you advice that so often the one-dimensional advisor misses.

Want What You Are Seeking

One morning, I saw a squirrel valiantly try to climb a pole upon which hung my bird feeder. After several minutes of struggling, this ambitious rodent finally reached the top, only to find that not only was the feeder weight-sensitive, it was filled with thistle—not a squirrel favorite. While I admired the fight in the little animal, it struck me as sad that he eventually would realize that what he was fighting for was not truly worth it.

I have clients who come into my office trying to figure out how they can afford to escape from the profession in which they have spent their lives. We all must do things that we don't particularly enjoy, but shouldn't our objective be to fill up our lives as much as possible with meaning, even at the expense of some financial success? Again from *Emerson*:

"I remember when I was a boy going upon the beach and being charmed with the color and forms of the shells. I picked many up and put them in my pocket. When I got home I could find nothing that I gathered, nothing but some dry ugly mussel and snail shells."

Don't fill your pockets with mussel and snail shells. Choose to do something of high impact every day. Maybe leave work a little earlier to do something special at home. Or maybe carve out a little of your take-home pay to give to charity or share your time to volunteer.

Be Where You Are

The most important thing I realized when birding was that I needed to pay attention to what I was doing right at the moment. My senses had to be operating on all cylinders so that I could react quickly to whatever was around me.

With money, we often get too far ahead of ourselves. If the market is bad, we think it will stay bad forever. If it is good, we think it will never end. We must look at each financial decision in the context of what we need to do right now in order to be in harmony with what matters to us. If you are maximizing the moment, the rest will take care of itself. If you are spending on things that matter and saving for things that matter, I guarantee that you will live a life that matters.

Any other type of life is for the birds.

SPEND YOUR LIFE WISELY.™
THIS COLUMN ORIGINALLY APPEARED IN THE MINNEAPOLIS *Star Tribune* ON JUNE 12, 2005.

Perfect Segue

When school ended, my family and I took an extended vacation. I want to share with you some of the tremendous financial-planning insights that I gained from this trip (as well as maybe create a way by which I can write some of the expenses off for taxes).

There I was, one early evening, lying on my back in front of a renowned museum. Before you develop this fantasy of me reclining on a grassy lawn contemplating great works of art, you need to know that I was actually lying in gravel, having been abruptly thrown off my rented Segway upright scooter. So I picked myself up, brushed off my clothes, and continued to tour, slightly battered.

Doesn't that sort of feel like the stock market this year? There we all were, riding effortlessly along and enjoying the seemingly irrepressible markets until we hit a rough patch in mid-May and ended up flat on our backs. Everything took a spill. It really didn't matter if we owned big stocks, small stocks, international stocks, growth stocks, or value stocks—nothing was working.

This will continue to be a real up-and-down year for U.S. stocks because of issues like interest rates, consumer confidence, the deficit, and energy prices. It will also be a pretty volatile year for international stocks because of issues related to the expansion of the European Union and its own stock market cycles. But if you don't need access to your money for at least three years, then you simply have to examine whether you are appropriately diversified and get back on the scooter.

Toward the end of our Segway tour, I heard a loud crash, followed by recurring smaller crashes. I looked over my shoulder to find my wife repeatedly smashing into a beautiful Aston-Martin (think Bond, James Bond) convertible. The nonplussed car owner was staring in shock as my wife (her bike helmet and scooter making her look like an extraterrestrial gone berserk) tried to get the vehicle back under control. But the turning mechanism of the scooter is located where a throttle would be on a motorcycle or Jet Ski, so slowing down is actually turning left. This counterintuitive control kept the Segway hammering into the car instead of coming to a stop.

How often do we find ourselves doing the same things over and over, even though we know that they are not working? Sometimes it feels as though any forward progress we make with our money or our lives is followed by the surprise expense that sets us back behind where we started. It's unrealistic to try to make dramatic changes, even though, logically, you know that you should. For example, if your budget feels out of control, don't think that you can suddenly shift to austerity—you will find yourself repeatedly slapping that credit card back on the counter. Instead, think of making small changes upon which you can build: one degree of one degree. And most important, when you do something that is consistent with your objectives, take a moment to give yourself the credit for doing so.

On our flight home, the airplane was delayed taking off because of bad weather in Minneapolis. When we finally did leave, the ride was pretty smooth until we started our descent. We hit such storms that the plane was bouncing around almost uncontrollably. The pilot ended up abandoning the Minneapolis arrival and diverting to Rochester, Minnesota. We had to decide whether to wait for a couple of hours for another plane or rent a car and drive back to Minneapolis. I took out my cell phone, called a rental agency, and got a car at the Rochester airport so that we could drive the hour and a half home, thankful to be on the ground.

How many times do our best-laid plans get diverted? We think that everything is going as planned and suddenly we hit some turbulence. We have several options when the bumps come. We could ignore them and just try to work harder, hoping that they will go away. While this head-in-the-sand approach sometimes can work, it does so only by accident. Another approach is to run from the bumps—turn around and wait for them to subside. The problem with this approach is that while you know that things will subside, you don't have much impact on when they stop. Sometimes inaction is the right choice, but it must be a conscious choice. The best approach is to look at the situation to determine what options are available and which ones give you the best chance of coming close to your true objectives.

Any of us can make great choices when we have all the information; taking action during periods of uncertainty, though, is where life's real opportunities lie. Sometimes we may get thrown for a loop, or feel like we are knocking our heads against a wall, or be forced to do things that we had never expected. The good life doesn't come from controlling how everything goes, but by appreciating how unpredictable it all is and being able to adapt.

SPEND YOUR LIFE WISELY.™

THIS COLUMN ORIGINALLY APPEARED IN THE MINNEAPOLIS *Star Tribune* ON JULY 16, 2006.

Spring for a Guide

As I munched on the beetle, I was thinking to myself about the trust I had in someone whom I had just met. Normally, I am not too big on eating bugs. As my children stared at me with a combination of awe and disgust (I was used to them looking at me with one of those two sentiments), I realized that I would never have tried this on my own. After only three days in Costa Rica, I was chomping away on an insect because our guide said it was fine to do so. I had built up enough confidence in him that I was administering a medical test on myself—to see if by eating this asthma beetle, I would actually feel my lungs open up. And you know what? They did.

We were spending two weeks in Costa Rica over spring break. Our hope was to see most of the country experientially. We wanted to be among the birds, insects, animals, and arachnids. I wanted to leave my office and the prospects of war far behind. Little did I know how much I would learn about financial planning.

Our guide, Adrian, met us at the airport and told us he was going to be with us for the first eight days of the trip. In a very short time, he had to gain the confidence of my wife and me, and, with far more difficulty, that of my daughters. He started by telling us things about Costa Rica, but he quickly evolved into asking us questions about the experiences that we wanted to have while in his country. He didn't tell us how qualified he was—he showed us by immersing us in all aspects of the trip. Most important, it was quickly apparent that his agenda was to ensure that he understood what we wanted and then make it happen.

Isn't that just like a first meeting with a financial planning client? When I started in this business, my initial meetings were almost always about proving what I knew rather than determining what the client really wanted. I had to camouflage my insecurity by talking about how different I was from other planners rather than having clients choose to work with me because it was clear that we had similar values. Clients expected me to be competent; they didn't expect me to be empathetic. I am reminded of one prospect who came to my office after meeting with another financial planner who had said he was the only financial planner around who invested tax-efficiently. Even if that were true, is that the distinguishing characteristic upon which you would want to build your practice? Wouldn't you rather be like Adrian, who offered what was best for us only after he found out what was best for us?

My daughters had a number of amazing experiences, including spending a day with a group of fifth-grade students from a school in Costa Rica who were on a field trip at one of the eco-lodges where we stayed. While the girls were doing that, my wife was set up in an Adirondack chair at the river's edge, completing a work assignment she brought along. I got to take a walk through the rain forest with Adrian—who gave me another lesson on financial planning.

One of the advantages of using a guide is that they see things we naturally miss. It may be because they look at things differently than we do. I may be looking for a bird, while he is looking for a rustling in the trees. I may be trying to see a viper, while he is looking for a habitat in which a viper would live. I guess I am looking for results, while he is knee-deep in process, with an eye on what's ahead.

This is the same as what we do in our business. Our clients may be looking for a top-performing mutual fund while we focus on what an appropriate investment policy needs to be to meet their goals. Our clients may be arguing about saving for retirement versus taking a family trip, while we steer them into understanding their motivations with each. Maybe a trip represents creating experiences that their family will share forever. Maybe saving for retirement is a way for them to feel like they are ensuring they will not be a burden to their children as they age. When we act as guides for our clients, we take the time to look at the habitat rather than just finding the snake.

As we continued to walk along the trails, Adrian was talking about the symbiotic relationship (yes, he used the word symbiotic) between everything that exists in the rain forest. How the fallen trees have lichens that fertilize the ground or provide food for some of the animals. How the animals and insects are independent of each other yet need each other in order to exist. Everything has a purpose and everything must give back.

Again, this spoke to me about our life's work. We help our clients see the relationship between their actions and the way their life works. We show them the inter-connectedness of their choices around how they work, how they spend time with their family, and how they spend or save their money. Through our emphasis on philanthropy, we help them see their place in the larger world. We help them define their purpose and decide how to give back.

The last part of our trip was without a guide, although we did have access to people who could take us bird-watching or hiking. It became a much different trip. Even though those guides were knowledgeable, our excursions were with groups. The walks were interest-ing, but not intimate; informative, but not personal. I couldn't help wondering, on some of our self-guided tours, what we might be missing. And all of us missed our new friend, Adrian.

People can choose to self-guide their financial plan-ning. People can choose to work with planners or pro-grams that don't necessarily understand their individual needs, but provide good general information. Both of those options can be better than doing nothing. But just as our trip was enriched by spending the money for a guide, who took care of us because he cared about us, our clients' lives are enriched through working with us. Is there an appropriate price tag for this? It just may be priceless.

SPEND YOUR LIFE WISELY.™

REPRINTED WITH PERMISSION BY THE FINANCIAL PLANNING ASSOCIATION, *Journal of Financial Planning*, JULY 2003, ROSS LEVIN, "FINANCIAL GUIDES."

For more information on the Financial Planning Association, please visit www.fpanet.org or call 1-800-322-4237.

Unpredictability

I can't go alone to the bathroom in my home anymore. Every time I head in that direction, our cat, Cozy, runs past me, jumps up on the sink, and screams for me to turn on the water faucet. Ever since I let her drink out of the sink she regards her own water bowl like a glass of Ripple at a wine tasting.

After reading Steven Levitt and Stephen Dubner's new book, *Super Freakonomics—Global Cooling, Patriotic Prostitutes, and Why Suicide Bombers Should Buy Life Insurance*, I think I understand why. People, and I guess cats, often respond to incentives in unpredictable ways. Or if they respond predictably, what happens may still be surprising. Using a format similar to the book's, I want to give you my own Freakonomics interpretation.

How is buying a home similar to kidnapping your former lover in France? A French singer earned a five-year prison sentence for capturing his former girlfriend. I was thinking that this guy's time served is about equivalent to how long you probably have to own a home before you can financially get out of it. This is important because with the tax credits available to first-time home buyers, many of our clients are thinking that this is a great chance to help their kids get into real estate.

It may or may not be. For those ready to make at least a five-year commitment, home ownership can be a wonderful thing. But the decision is more complicated than simply comparing rental costs and mortgage costs. First, home ownership expenses are greater than your monthly payment. Not only do you have the regular costs of heat, electricity, waste removal, etc., but you also have those extra unexpected costs—furnace, roof, water softener. If you help your child with the big purchase, be prepared to have a plan for all the things that you probably didn't factor in.

Second, and I think more important, home ownership limits flexibility. In this environment, some people can't move elsewhere for work because they are stuck with a home they can't sell. Young people tend to be very mobile. Owning a home before they are set in a career could end up costing them a lot of money by forcing them to stay with a job that they don't love or by not allowing them to pursue something different and potentially more lucrative.

Third, buying your first home is one of the major rites of passage to adulthood. It may seem like a wonderful thing to help your child achieve this, but it may be depriving them of something that they really want to achieve on their own. Helping your kids get a home that is more than they can afford changes many things. It may put them in a neighborhood with people who are in a different financial situation. It may make it difficult for them to properly maintain their property. It may prevent them from being able to do things they would otherwise want to experience if they didn't feel so tied down.

How is paying taxes like eating dessert?

Sweets, in moderation, are fine. But some people avoid them entirely, and some gorge on them until they feel sick. This is sort of like taxes. There is some amount of taxes that we all should pay. Above a certain level, taxes can be unproductive. That band, though, is probably wider than what many people think and not as wide as some people want.

Taxes often represent, as explained in *Super Freakonomics*, a "principal-agent problem [where] two parties in a given undertaking seem to have the same incentives, but in fact may not." Taxes are paid to provide services. The problem is that we all don't want the same services in the same amounts. This automatically makes tax policy incendiary.

But we have clients who take the abstinence approach to taxes: They don't sell investments that they should because that would trigger taxable gains, they take on more debt than appropriate because they get a tax benefit and they even sock away more money for retirement than needed because the government is subsidizing it. You should still do appropriate planning, but rather than try to avoid the inevitable, it is far better to integrate it into the decisions that will make you the happiest.

There may be a tax cost for this, but sometimes it's worth it. And paying it usually is better than owning a home you don't want in a tax haven where you don't want to live.

SPEND YOUR LIFE WISELY.™

THIS COLUMN ORIGINALLY APPEARED IN THE MINNEAPOLIS *Star Tribune* ON NOVEMBER 28, 2009.

Timing the Market

Had I been better at interviewing, I would be single and still trying to figure out what type of work I should be doing.

When I applied to be an orientation leader at the University of Minnesota my sophomore year in college, I didn't get the job. I was crestfallen. I got it the next year, though. And as luck (or randomness) would have it, my future wife also got the job. So did the future wife of my future business partner.

So here I am, 28 years after the fact, looking at my pretty good life, and thinking if I had only been a little bit more articulate, a wee bit more convincing, a tiny bit more passionate, my life may not have turned out nearly so well.

In *The Drunkard's Walk—How Randomness Rules Our Lives*, Prof. Leonard Mlodinow says:

> "When we look back in detail on the major events of our lives, it is not uncommon to be able

to identify seemingly inconsequential random events that led to big changes."

This makes sense as we retrospectively focus on what happened, but this also is true about what never happened. For example, we don't know if the wrong turn we took helped us avoid an accident. In the field of financial planning, I think about these things all the time.

One of my clients called in March to tell me of his retired neighbor who had sold out of everything right before the market fell last fall. This incredibly prescient person was planning to sit on the sidelines until the Dow fell to a certain level. She would then venture back in. While I have a great relationship with my client, I don't think he was telling me this anecdote simply to have a conversation. Unstated, but implied, was: "How come a smart professional like you didn't sell everything at the same time she did?"

So, is this an example of my idiocy or her brilliance—or both? Or neither?

From Mlodinow:

"Random events often look like non-random events, and in interpreting human affairs we must take care not to confuse the two."

In order to understand whether this neighbor was an undiscovered Warren Buffett, citing this one market call is not sufficient. In fact, uncovering several correct market decisions may not be enough. If you look at the universe of investors, basic probability teaches us that someone is going to make great market calls several times in a row simply by chance. The problem for any of us is determining when these market calls are inspired or lucky.

So now what?

Since March, the Federal Reserve had continued to cut interest rates, and the markets had been up double digits from their lows. Because the Dow never hit this neighbor's reentry point, she is sitting on a pile of cash that (because of that sneaky Fed) is earning less and less. So now what does she do? Stick to her guns or bite the bullet? This week, the Fed is meeting again, and there's speculation that it will either hold rates where they are or raise them in response to growing inflation.

This is not to say that the market won't fall from here—rest assured that it will. But know that it will go up from here, too. This is simply to say that if you are investing your money for a period of more than three years, it is foolish to be trying to time getting in and out because there are so many random variables that cause short-term volatility. But equally silly is to be invested all in one type of investment—be it an index fund or a hedge fund—because of those same variables.

Stocks are always priced on some vision of the future. Day-to-day, emotional responses cause prices to move up and down. But over the long run, stocks move in particular directions because of the underlying strength or weakness in the companies. Think about it as the difference between weather and climate change. Just because it is colder this year than last year does not mean that the ozone layer has stayed intact. The weather changes all the time for varied reasons; the question to answer is what is the long-term direction?

Large stocks, small stocks, growth stocks, value stocks, U.S. stocks, and international stocks all move upward over long periods of time because economies grow over time. But they are mispriced daily. Eventually, they move back in line. This is based on the scientific principle pointed out by Mlodinow that "processes that [do] not exhibit regression toward the mean would eventually go out of control."

That is partly why growth stocks got crushed early in the decade. It also is why you want to invest in multiple asset classes and rebalance your winners back to your losers.

Beyond the market, randomness is everywhere we look. You can improve your chances for better outcomes through multiple attempts at the things that are important to you. Had I not gone back to apply for that orientation-leader job again, you would probably not be reading about my wife, our twins, and my business in these monthly columns.

SPEND YOUR LIFE WISELY.™
THIS COLUMN ORIGINALLY APPEARED IN THE MINNEAPOLIS *Star Tribune* ON JUNE 22, 2008.

Biography

Ross Levin, CFP®
FOUNDING PRINCIPAL AND PRESIDENT

Ross Levin is the Founding Principal and President of Accredited Investors Inc. His book, *The Wealth Management Index*, published by McGraw-Hill/Irwin, provides a framework for advisors to assess and manage their clients' plans and goals. He launched the CCH Journal of Retirement Planning and served as Editor for two years. He is a regular columnist for the *Journal of Financial Planning* and the *Star Tribune*. Mr. Levin is a sought after speaker on financial matters.

Mr. Levin is a CERTIFIED FINANCIAL PLANNER™ practitioner certified by the Certified Financial Planner Board of Standards in Denver, Colorado. He received a BSB from the University of Minnesota, and is a nationally recognized expert in financial planning, appearing in numerous publications, including: *The Wall Street Journal, Business Week, Fortune, The New York Times, Newsweek, Barron's, Money Magazine,* as well as on television and radio shows nationally, such as NBC Nightly News, The Oprah Winfrey Show, CBS This Morning, and American Public Media's Marketplace Money. He was named one of the top financial planners nationally by *Money Magazine, Worth Magazine, Mutual Funds Magazine,* and *Medical Economics.* He was a featured advisor in Mary Rowland's book published by Bloomberg *Best Practices for Financial Advisors.* He was named by *Financial Planning Magazine* as one of the five most influential people in financial planning and by *Investment Advisor Magazine* as one of the twenty-five most influential individuals in and around the advisory profession. He was the first recipient of the Financial Planning Association's Heart of Financial Planning Award.

Mr. Levin served as Chairman of the International Association for Financial Planning, which is now the FPA, an organization of over 28,000 financial service professionals. He also has served on the Board of Governors for the CFP® Board of Standards in Denver, Colorado.

He lives in Minneapolis with his wife and twin daughters.

Mr. Levin can be reached at ross@accredited.com

Certified Financial Planner Board of Standards Inc. owns the certification marks CFP®, CERTIFIED FINANCIAL PLANNER™ and federally registered CFP (with flame design) in the U.S., which it awards to individuals who successfully complete CFP Board's initial and ongoing certification requirements.

General Reading List

Books on Financial Planning, Economics, and Investments

The Myth of the Rational Market - Justin Fox

The Black Swan - Nassim Nicholas Taleb

Capital Ideas - Peter Bernstein

The Intelligent Investor - Benjamin Graham (edited by Jason Zweig)

A Random Walk Down Wall Street - Burton Malkiel

New Ideas from Dead Economists - Todd Buchholz

The Mind of the Market - Michael Shermer

Your Money and Your Brain - Jason Zweig

Fooled by Randomness - Nassim Nicholas Taleb

How Markets Fail - John Cassidy

Common Stocks and Uncommon Profit - Philip A. Fisher

Stocks for the Long Run - Jeremy Siegel

When Genius Failed - Roger Lowenstein

Why Smart People Make Big Money Mistakes and How to Correct Them - Gary Belsky and Thomas Gilovich

Freakonomics and *Super Freakonomics* - Steven D. Levitt and Stephen J. Dubner

Asset Allocation - Roger Gibson

The New Frugality - Chris Farrell

Your Money Life - Ruth Hayden

Prodigal Sons and Material Girls: How Not to be Your Child's ATM -Nathan Dungan

Books on Money & Meaning

The Richest Man in Babylon – George S. Clason

Nudge – Richard Thaler and Cass Sunstein

The Next 100 Years: A Forecast for the 21st Century – George Friedman

Stumbling on Happiness – Daniel Todd Gilbert

The Paradox of Choice: Why More Is Less – Barry Schwartz

Thanks!: How Practicing Gratitude Can Make You Happier – Robert Emmons

The Science of Fear: Why We Fear the Things We Shouldn't--and Put Ourselves in Greater Danger – Daniel Gardner

Money and the Meaning of Life – Jacob Needleman

Destructive Emotions - Daniel Goleman and the Dalai Lama

Lovingkindness – Sharon Salzberg

Care of the Soul – Thomas Moore

The Heart Aroused: Poetry and the Preservation of the Soul in Corporate America – David Whyte

Forgive for Good – Fred Luskin

How to Stop Worrying and Start Living (Revised Edition) – Dale Carnegie

Siddhartha – Herman Hesse

True Success – Thomas Morris

The Good Life: Truths That Last in Times of Need – Reverend Peter Gomes

Let Your Life Speak – Parker Palmer

Encore – Marc Freedman

Lifecraft – F. Forrester Church

Home Economics – Wendell Berry

What Matters Most – James Hollis

Happiness – Matthieu Ricard

If Only - Neal Roese

Books Mentioned

Now, Discover Your Strengths - Marcus Buckingham and Donald O. Clifton

How to Stop Worrying and Start Living (Revised Edition) - Dale Carnegie

Thanks!: How Practicing Gratitude Can Make You Happier - Robert Emmons

Why Smart Executives Fail: And What You Can Learn from Their Mistakes - Sydney Finkelstein

The Sermon on the Mount: The Key to Success in Life - Emmet Fox

The Next 100 Years: A Forecast for the 21st Century - George Friedman

The Science of Fear: Why We Fear the Things We Shouldn't--and Put Ourselves in Greater Danger - Daniel Gardner

Stumbling on Happiness - Daniel Todd Gilbert

The Good Life: Truths That Last in Times of Need - Reverend Peter Gomes

Siddhartha - Herman Hesse

The Kite Runner - Khaled Hosseini

Leading from Within: Poetry That Sustains the Courage to Lead - Sam M. Intrator and Megan Scribner

The Drunkard's Walk: How Randomness Rules Our Lives - Leonard Mlodinow

The Heart of the Buddha's Teaching - Thich Nhat Hanh

A Whole New Mind: Moving from the Information Age to the Conceptual Age - Daniel H. Pink

Emerson: The Mind on Fire - Robert D. Richardson, Jr.

The Four Agreements: A Practical Guide to Personal Freedom, A Toltec Wisdom Book - Don Miguel Ruiz

The Paradox of Choice: Why More Is Less - Barry Schwartz

Authentic Happiness: Using the New Positive Psychology to Realize Your Potential for Lasting Fulfillment - Martin E. P. Seligman

DisneyWar - James B. Stewart

The Power of Now: A Guide to Spiritual Enlightenment - Eckhart Tolle

Bonds That Make Us Free: Healing Our Relationships, Coming to Ourselves - C. Terry Warner

The Heart Aroused: Poetry and the Preservation of the Soul in Corporate America - David Whyte